From B to A

Beta to Alpha

Hacking the flow state in

love, life, work and parenting.

Thomas Schorr-kon

*with much love &
thanks to you !
x x x x x*

T. R.

DEDICATION

This book is dedicated to the curious, to all those forever
questioning.

CONTENTS

ACKNOWLEDGMENTS

Firstly I must acknowledge my teacher Tom Brown Jr as the technique I have developed has grown out of the many things I learned from him. I would also like to acknowledge the ground breaking work of Mihaly Csikszentmihalyi that features in the book. I acknowledge my three progeny and our many adventures together. I would like to also acknowledge Ariel Grace as many of the insights about relationship arose during our time journeying together. I would also like to acknowledge Gregory Sams help with editing. Also Daniel Wagner who came up with the title.

1

FROM B TO A

NATURAL VS NORMAL

We have all felt moments when we are in the flow. Perhaps it is when we are playing sport and everything is just going our way and then we think "this is great, I am doing it perfectly", it is at this point we trip over or make a crucial error.

It could be that we are playing music or painting and we look at the time and find that what we thought was a few minutes has become hours as we have become so adsorbed in what we are doing. There are times when we are feeling exhausted at the end of a long day then we get in to the flow of cooking, or some creative task or a great conversation and our energy returns and carries us late in to the night. Sometimes we have days when we show up in the right place at the right time, and synchronicities seem to be happening. There are also times when we miss certain disastrous events because we are staying calm and in the flow. There might be times when we are in a wood or by a lake and find a sense of deep connection with nature. As that universal connection is felt and the peace and gratitude that can accompany it takes hold, we may notice the birds singing around us or a deer looking at us with curiosity rather than fear. It could be that we are so adsorbed in our activity of choice that we are able to still the mind while we practice the activity. Thus removing us from the feelings of stress enough for us to deal with whatever the issues we are facing more skilfully.

These are all occurrences that we might recognise as they are natural, because the flow state is our natural state and therefore accessible to all of us. This book is about accessing this state when we choose, simply and naturally and making use of the many benefits that it brings.

The Alpha state which is one of the four main brainwave states that were discovered when E.E.G. machines (Electro Encephalograph) were developed. Gamma the fifth state was only discovered when the move was made from analogue E.E.G. machines to digital. The brainwave state that is considered normal for humans is called the Beta state, this state is a faster speed at which the brain is operating. When the Beta state becomes the norm is as we move in to puberty and become self-conscious, it is at this point we start to make comparisons between ourselves and others, when we have to start to construct a way of interfacing with the world. It is also when our mind starts to develop a state of self-conflict. This is in the form of unsolicited thoughts arising as a continuous experience. We are also in the process of encountering our emotional selves. This combination of powerful mental, emotional and chemical change that is taking place simultaneously is a lot to process. At the same time there is also a questioning of the cultural stories and boundaries that comes in to play. Questions about what is going on beyond the physical become uppermost. There is a massive change taking place in the individual questions of control and mastery of the, at times, extreme states. Understanding what is being experienced becomes imperative. Yet relying on the current cultural role models that are available it is all too easy for the young person to be left feeling empty and alone. This can leads to experimentation with drugs amongst other things, in an attempt to find answers or just to experience something else. With an understanding of the states they are moving through a lot of the problems our youth are experiencing can be resolved.

Even as adults we may not have managed to master our own state in a way that does away with worry, stress, reactiveness and gives us access to greater energy, creativity, connection and peace. If as teenagers we had learned this perhaps we could pass on our understanding to our offspring.

Of the four main brainwave states, the flow state which is a state of calm and focus is the closest to the natural earth resonance. The natural earth resonance is called the Schuman resonance after the physicist who discovered it this will be explained later in detail. Living with a strong connection to nature and the natural frequency is both invigorating and inspiring. It can keep us remain sane in an upside down world. When we are tuned in to the Alpha state and are in nature then we start to experience the natural world as if we were invisible to the birds and animals. This is a deeply nourishing experience and when we become adept we can access this state even in the middle of the city.

The benefits of the Alpha state include a long list and within this frequency range there are many aspects we can access that can enhance our lives.

Access:

Flow state

Being in the zone

Recalling memories

Accomplishing difficult tasks body control

Creativity

Inner guidance

Unity consciousness

Energy

Primal self

Master your energy

Stills the mind

Connects us with nature

Calms stress

Conflict resolution reduces inner conflict

Problem solving

Two minutes of practice is the equivalent of an hour's meditation

Access to the Alpha faster than the science says is possible.

The simplest and quickest way to access meditative stillness.

There are several ways in which I have gained access to the flow state throughout my life. I have always painted and trained as a fine artist. I began an exploration of the martial arts as a child and began to meditate around the age of 14. Each of these practices gave me access to the flow state in different ways and has different beneficial outcomes.

The physical movement practice allows the stresses of the day to be put down, left outside the dojo, so that the mind can be brought in to the body. This creates a quality of synchronisation between mind and body that gives access to the flow. Within the karate dojo, there is also the possibility that if there is no synchronization or body control then one may get woken up by some kind of physical test of presence. The forms of sparing and touching hands are specifically orientated towards encouraging full presence.

Working with the creative self brings a deep inner connection, the capacity to touch on deep emotion and transform it. The act of exploring different media also creates a level of immersion in the process that drops us directly in to the flow. I found that to maintain this capacity once I had children required the breaking down of my process in to small sections so I could drop in to that immersive state for short periods as and when the time became available.

The practice of meditation seemed to slow down my mind, helped me to see my thoughts as unwanted guests that for a very long time I housed happily, as they passed through the guest house of my mind. The time spent trying to do nothing as it was in the beginning always left me feeling refreshed, even though it was mostly a wrestling match with my mind. I was held in one of two main wrestling holds, one that criticized and disparaged me and the other that held me up as special and angelic. It became clear over time that both positions were equally unhelpful. The training of my body to remain still, to sit, was helpful. Over time more space came between the experience of self and thought or feeling. I followed a guru at one point until I was cured of gurus by a certain Rinpoche, who helped me realise that we are the ones who need to tread the path, do the work and that the path is unique for each of us.

The states that the meditation helped develop were sometimes Alpha and sometimes deeper states. But during this period there was no map, no way of accessing the potential of these states, very little understanding of how to work the vehicle that is meditation. All of the meditation techniques I encountered were focused on going with in, and one of the things I observed in those who had been on the path for long periods was a crystallisation of the exterior egoic self.

It was in my late twenties that I came across ways to access the Alpha state in nature and meditation that was as much focused on the inner realms as the realms of nature. A friend pointed me towards a particular author - Tom Brown Jr. I had read Carlos Castaneda and many other such writings - when I found the Tracker many things changed in my life.

My first experience of accessing Alpha in nature happened after reading one of Tom's manuals about how to move silently and invisibly in nature. Whilst running on the outskirts of Bristol I decided to try out some of the techniques I had been reading about. I began to use what he called splatter vision and fox walking and after taking about ten steps I met a fox head on. This was not a usual occurrence for me back then and it made me realise something was happening that I needed to know more about.

Fast forward to ten years in to my training and teaching, I set up a school to teach survival skills, nature connection and shamanism in 1995 and as anyone who teaches knows there is as much learning through teaching as there is when we are a student. Especially if we continue to test what we know and run experiments to build on our experience.

One of the major lessons that we were taught implicitly was to work with what inspired us. Anything that did not work that we had been taught was to be discarded. The only problem I have found with this is that everything I have learned from Tom Brown Jr has worked. From the skill of rubbing sticks together to make fire to accessing the furthest reaches of the spiritual realms. It is hard for me to say this about all of my teachers. The important premise is, 'Do not believe anything written here, as that is lazy. Run your own experiments and rely on your own results'. Your results are the single most important information that you have access to. This becomes your area of knowledge, not belief but hard won understanding from running your own experiments. This builds awareness which becomes presence.

It was whilst teaching stalking that I began to observe interesting phenomena. Stalking in nature is required to hunt and to move without being detected, a skill that if we were living close to the earth we all would have been schooled in as our survival and that of the tribe would have been dependent on it. Stalking is moving at around one minute per step. For most people living a western lifestyle this is a complex endeavour. Slow movement requires a lot of body control and awareness.

WE WANT TO KILL SOMETHING

I remember one particular incident twenty years ago I was assisting in a mentoring experiment. Ten boys of mixed ethnic backgrounds who had been excluded from schools in the St Paul's area of London were to be mentored by ten mentors in a beautiful centre in Wales.

I had arrived with my own agenda and realised that that made at least ten different agendas. So I decided on the first evening to drop my agenda and just let things take their own course. I explained to the young men my skill set and left it to them to come and find me if they wanted to engage.

One afternoon two of the boys came up to me and said "We want to go in to the woods and kill something!" Without any hesitation I agreed and we set off in to the woods finding throwing stick as deadly projectiles as we went.

We walked through the woods for a good twenty minutes without seeing any wildlife. I asked them 'have you seen anything?' They both said no, 'How stupid of me I said I should have shown you how to move silently and invisibly' Then I suggested we try using peripheral vision and fox walking, the boys got it fairly swiftly and we proceeded to move through the forest still not encountering anything but this time we moved more slowly stopping periodically to listen and scan the woods. The boys had begun to quieten down. Another half an hour passed as we went deeper in to the forest and again I asked 'Have you seen anything?' They both replied that they had seen nothing. Again I feigned stupidity: 'Perhaps it is too noisy in your mind and that is disturbing the animals in the environment' I suggested. They both affirmed that it was noisy in their minds. We were stood on the edge of a beautiful glade and I suggested they sit and I would show them how to quieten their mind. We sat quietly for a short while and then I took them in to a relaxing meditative state. We sat for a further half an hour at the end of which both boys were in a deep Alpha state. By this time it was getting to late afternoon and we needed to head back as we had come quite a way in to the forest.

On the walk back they began to enjoy just being in the woods, noticing various plants and beautiful sights. As we returned we came across a sheep in the woods but the blood lust had gone replaced with a quiet appreciation. We made our way back to the centre as the sun was setting, we came to a gap in the trees and I paused to take in the sunset and one of them said, 'isn't that beautiful.'

These two young men had moved from the desire to kill something to a state of inner peace and gratitude. I had only done what they had asked and taught them what was necessary to get close to any animals through the practice of stalking.

Hunting as it was practiced in the past would have required this type of tempering of our young people. They all would have had the understanding of how to quiet the mind and move without disturbing the natural world. As we no longer have the imperative to hunt or evade our enemies these natural skills have been lost. This is one of the integral natural skills that allow a level of connection with nature that's absence can cause a deep and strong feeling of separation.

STALKING

The first time I experienced stalking was at the Tracker school. There were around a hundred students all learning this ancient and much misunderstood practice. We began by fox walking and using our peripheral vision. A fox walk is a natural way of placing the foot and this process changes what we are experiencing both internally and externally. Externally it felt to me like suddenly there were only a handful of people there rather than a hundred. It was a bizarre experience and internally things quietened down, I felt calm and focused-less thought was bothering me.

THE NATURAL STEP

In order to experience the natural step it is helpful to relax the ankle. If you stand on one leg lifting your other leg and shake your ankle, it relaxes. Then allow the foot to meet the ground. It is important that the ankle is actually relaxed; you will notice this is happening when the foot is soft and no longer held at a ninety degree angle. The foot will meet the ground in a very different way to the way that you have been used to stepping. What will happen is that the outside edge of the foot will meet the ground first then the foot will roll across from small toe to the large toe as opposed to the heel striking the ground first. This brings with it a great deal of benefit.

The first benefit for the Stalker is that it reduces the amount of sound that is made as the foot hits the ground secondly it allows much more control so that if we do begin to make a sound we can stop the sound being made halfway through. We are also employing the full use of all of the bone structures that exist in the foot. If we take all of the bones of the hands and feet and put them together they add up to almost half the bones in the entire body. The bone structures of the feet are designed to absorb a great deal of shock including an entire life time of walking and running. If we walk normally wearing shoes with the foot striking the ground with our heel then we miss the capacity of our body to absorb a vast amount of the shock of each step. This can cause injury to our bodies over time.

As well as placing the foot more naturally we were encouraged to use our eyes differently, with a softer gaze more naturally. This wide angle vision or peripheral vision makes a tremendous difference to what we are looking at and what is happening in us.

WIDE EYEDED

The gateway to this is in using our eyes in a different way to the normal way we are used to. What is considered the normal way of looking at the world is typically using a very narrow focus of vision. This is largely how predators view the world: eyes front, assessing possible targets, ranges and striking distances. This is not to say we are all in a predatory mind set yet we are all moving from one image to another as we go through the day. The introduction of more and more viewing screens has only served to reinforce this way of diminishing our potential capacity to use our vision in a more powerful way.

It is our peripheral vision that we need to expand and use more, this is sometimes called wide-angle vision. There are a few groups of people who employ their peripheral vision more than most: battle-hardened veterans, martial artists and I suspect some sportsmen and women. It has been scientifically proven that women have much greater peripheral vision than men which puts men at a great disadvantage in respect of shifting into a more intuitive state which is the state that this shift in the use of the eyes can help to create.

There are a number of things that change when we move into using our peripheral vision not just our capacity to take in more visual information. It affects our depth of field, night vision, and state of consciousness, measurably changing our brainwave state.

CONES AND RODS

Our eyes have two different types of cells, cones and rods and as we move into peripheral vision we start to use the rods more than the cones. The rods are more sensitive to light so we find that our night vision is increased when in peripheral vision. Because we are not so focused on a particular object or target, our depth of field becomes limitless, allowing us to perceive movement beyond the first layer of undergrowth that our eye would normally rest on if we were using our predatory vision. Our attention shifts from paying attention to objects to our attention being drawn by movement. In fact we become hypersensitive to tiny movements which will draw our attention in a way that makes us far more aware of what is going on around us than if we were stuck in our predatory vision. The peripheral vision is more like the vision of most prey animals who are paying a wider attention to the environment because their lives to depend on it.

PREDATOR AND PREY VISION

The position of our eyes is an indication of the primary way they are intended to be used. Humans are the number one predator on the planet and so our tendency is to use the focused forward vision the position of our eyes predicates. This means we are set up to act and look as predators. Most prey animals have their eyes set on either side of their head in order to be able to keep themselves safe. If we compare the skull of a deer, a prey animal, and the skull of predators such as a fox or cat this becomes very evident. Prey animal's vision is based on detecting movement and less emphasis is placed on finding the exact location of a target. With the position of a prey animal's eyes they are in a constant peripheral type of vision. When we use peripheral vision we become more sensitive to tiny movements and our depth of field changes from the first specific target to infinity. So we can see the similarity between prey vision and our use of peripheral vision.

This is backed up by our own experiences of having the capacity to feel when someone is staring at us (using predatory vision) from behind or above. We all have had experiences of either staring at someone and them turning round to look at us or vice versa.

It is as if when we use our predatory vision we are directing a beam of a powerful light focused on what we are looking at, which can be felt by the person or animal in the beam. When we look at people and animals with wide angle vision that beam is diffused and it is felt less. The predatory focus is removed and the observed is left more at ease. This becomes the doorway to invisibility. This is because our presence is felt less.

NATURE AS MIRROR

The world that we live in is a huge biofeedback mechanism. When our brainwave state is resonant with the natural state the birds and animals suddenly perceive us as one of them rather than as separate. Human behaviour in nature, if it is the same as it is in an urban environment, is not understood by the birds and animals, it is felt as threatening. Therefore they respond in fearful ways making alarm calls, falling silent or flying away screaming. This means that the natural world is reflecting us back to ourselves. Showing us where we are in ourselves like a giant natural mirror.

If we enter a natural environment and sit quietly for half an hour the area will return to its natural baseline and we may well be able to experience signs of things returning to normal through birds feeding, singing very close to us perhaps right next to us, this will then signal to the other animals, the mammals that it is safe and we might be lucky enough to see a wood mouse run across our foot or have a squirrel drop a nut on us.

The study of the alarm system of nature suddenly opens up to us as we begin to develop our capacity to stalk. A deep connection starts to form within us as we experience nature undisturbed and up close, perhaps for the first time. This also starts to offer us a repeatable practice or way to be in nature that unlocks her hidden secrets.

Unlike the results of normal human activity where the birds fly screaming away from behaviours that they do not understand, thus alerting any animals in the vicinity that humans are coming (and we have to remember that we are the number one predator on the planet). We are already able to become more at one with our environment merely by slowing down and acting in a more natural way.

If we are hurrying, busy in our minds we are barely present in the place that we are in. We have brought with us all of the stress and worry from the city into the countryside. This internal disturbance is at odds with the natural rhythm of the earth and stands out like splashing loudly in a quiet pond. When we are quieter internally and are putting out fewer internal and external signals that create less ripples around us, the natural feedback we get further opens our heart as we witness first hand a bird singing or feeding its young or some other miraculous natural event.

There are many different stalking steps and what I have described is not really a stalking step it is merely a natural way of moving which should take place at perhaps half the pace that one would normally walk at.

When working with inner city kids I have found that teaching them the rudiments of silent and invisible movement or stalking helps to create an internal shift that makes them more receptive and able to engage. It has a calming and centring effect that makes it possible to work with some of the most difficult-to-reach students.

NATURAL LISTENING

These approaches form part of the skills of nature connection, both the way of moving and the awareness of how the ripples from our action flow out in to the pond of nature that surrounds us. Stalking is learning how to move causing few or no ripples, while reading the ripples that are being caused by other animals or people in the environment. These aspects translate in to any environment. For example the way people respond to us, the base line sounds of a class room or office. The scene in a movie when someone enters the bar and it goes silent and as the audience we know there is going to be trouble.

I remember when my first son was two, there were moments when he would go completely silent, moments that I listened for, as he was usually up to some mischief. A general level of noise indicated he was busy in a natural way, but the silences only came when he was trying some experiment that was going to have repercussions.

This aspect of nature listening extends beyond the voices of the birds. Each tree makes a different sound when the wind blows through it, water makes is its own music when it is flowing, and there are many types of rain that sound different, certain times of year have different sounds. This is expressed through the migratory birds as well as the difference between the seasonal conditions; the silence of snow, the raucous crackle of leaves in autumn, the still silent moments of summer, the awakening of the birds in spring.

During my teaching of stalking over twenty years I witnessed an interesting phenomenon that occurred almost every time. What I have found is that as people stalk when they reach minutes six the birds in the forest will for the first time come close to the students and start to sing in the trees directly around the whole group. I know it is minute six as I am carefully counting them through one minute per step for ten minutes.

This is the natural bio-feedback mechanism natures mirror expressing a feeling of safety around the humans practising their stalking. This is not random as I have witnessed this many times.

I have only had one class in twenty three years where the birds came and sang around the whole group at the beginning of the class.

WAVES

Several things are taking place that are useful to explain more precisely. The first is that the process of slowing down using the key aspects of stalking i.e. wide angle vision and stalking steps, entrains the brain in to an Alpha state the slowing down process also creates greater heart coherence. These are both electromagnetic shifts in the body. These shifts bring the person both in to an Alpha brain wave state the natural state for humans and this helps their brain waves match the natural electromagnetic rhythm of Nature.

Understanding how the brain waves function can help us get a scientific picture of what is going on. Brain waves have been studied since the 1920's and have been measureable since the invention of the EEG (electric encephalograph) around 70 years ago. Scientists have been using this technology to map brain wave states. So a great deal of research has been done in to brain wave states and this has more recently been taken up by the field of neuro science. The best description of brain waves I have come across is by

Ben Fuchs:

"Like all waves, the ones produced by the brain ebb and flow. Electrical bursts "fire" and then cease firing, essentially blinking on and off. The amount of times a burst of brain electricity and its subsequent cessation, turn on and off in every second is called a "cycle" and measured as "cycles-per-second" (CPS). The number of cycles-per-second is referred to as the "frequency". One that fires and stops firing, or cycles once a second, is said to have a frequency of one. If flow and ebb occurs twice a second the frequency would be two….and so on"

Through EEG measurements a spectrum of brain wave states have been measured and identified from 0.5 cycles per second up to 100's of cycles per second. We are going to shine a light just on a small part of the spectrum for the moment to help to understand what is going on when we are stalking.

EARTH'S NATURAL RESONANCE

As well as the brain having electromagnetic pulses or waves the whole of nature also is resonating in a similar way and it has been suggested by Hainsworth that our brain wave patterns have evolved from the electromagnetic resonance of the earth which is produced by the clouds.

Nature's electromagnetic resonance was discovered by Winfried Otto Schumann in 1952, but not until 1960-1963 was this finally measured by **Balser and Wagner** and Schumann's calculations and theories borne out. The earth's natural resonance was measured to be 7.83 hz. (Hertz are a measure of the number of cycles per second) (You might consider putting 'nature' as 'Nature' all through this. A bit German but like 'God'

The Schumann resonance is caused by the discharge of global lightning strikes with some 2000 thunderstorms globally discharging around 50 lightning strikes per storm. This electromagnetic energy is then resonated between the earth surface and the ionosphere to create a resonance that of 7.83 Hz this has a diurnal fluctuation of about + or - 0.5hz moving it between the Alpha frequency in the day and the Theta frequency at night. Alpha is between 8-12 Hz. And the Theta frequency is between 4-8 Hz. Schumann's calculation was taking the electromagnetic energy which is measured by the speed of light and dividing it by the circumference of the earth.

So when our own brain wave frequency is at the alpha level we resonate with the natural frequency of the earth. When the waves in our pond match the waves that are resonant around us then there is a connection a correlation, like a radio tuning in to a particular station we can receive and be received by others in this resonance.

All of nature is tuned to this resonance and so when we are in an Alpha state nature's feedback systems (the birds and animals) recognises us as part of nature and treat and respond to us as if we are part of and not separate or a threat.

Nature can also induct us in to these brainwave states when we spend time in nature especially when we are on our own. Interestingly if we are isolated from this rhythm we can suffer serious mental and physical health problems. This was discovered when astronauts first started to travel beyond the ionosphere.

"studies show that subjects living in isolation from geomagnetic rhythms over long periods of time developed increasing irregularities and chaotic physiological rhythms - which were dramatically restored after the introduction of a very weak 10Hz electrical field. Early astronauts suffered until SR (Schumann Resonance) generators were installed in their space crafts.

Ben Lonetree

By 1974 Ludwig had developed the first Schumann Resonance product that was installed in all space crafts by N.A.S.A. The installation of Schuman Resonance generators in all space craft demonstrates a clear scientific recognition of the importance of the Earth's natural resonance on its inhabitants and their wellbeing. .

What Ludwig also found was that while it was easy to measure the Schumann resonance in nature and on the ocean, it was difficult to measure it in cities. This was because of the increased number of electromagnetic waves generated by human's electronic devices. Perhaps the Schumann resonance technology could be employed in our inner cities to reduce stress and behavioural problems by reintroducing the natural Earth resonance.

THE HISTORY OF CLOUDS

When we understand that with the diurnal variation of 0.5 the Schumann resonance is moving between two resonances that relate directly to our own brain wave states. When we are in sleep we produce a Theta resonance. The range of Theta is from 4 Hz to 8 and Alpha from 8 to 12.

Hainsworth theorised that it is the Schumann resonance that has established our brainwave states. When we consider the reverence with which lightning wielding entities have been accorded through history. We find in many cultures a deification of this elemental power. In the Lakota tradition of North America they are known as the 'thunder beings,' in Norse mythology as Thor and Odin, and in Greek mythology as Zeus, Indra in Hinduism, and Shango in the Yoruba religion. This perhaps helps us to understand that the elemental forces, whether we personify them or not, are higher powers that influence our behaviour. We are not acting in the isolated fashion we would like to believe. Even our brain waves are connected to the energy of all things.

ENTRAINMENT

Having watched my students take their first stalking steps many times over the past 20 years I had noticed that at minute six the birds will come near the students and start singing in the trees around them for the first time since they have been in the woods for at least twenty four hours.

This left me with the question why six minutes?

My hypothesis so far is that when we slow down to stalking speed and use peripheral vision our brain slows to the Alpha brain wave rhythm. When this rhythm matches the Schuman resonance, the birds respond with their normal behaviour as if we were no longer perceived as predators. This is effectively being invisible to the natural alarm system of the forest.

What is left to figure out is the six minutes that it takes for the birds to respond to the group of students that have merged with the Schuman resonance.

What I discovered is that when we entrain the brain in to different states there is a certain time period that this takes.

"Entrainment" is a term from physics which means "the tendency for two vibrating bodies to lock into phase so that they vibrate in harmony".

For example, one tuning fork when struck and placed next to another tuning fork will cause the second one to vibrate at the same rate.
This was first observed by Dutch scientist, Christian Huygens, in 1665 while he was working on the design of the pendulum clock. He found that when he placed two of the clocks on a wall near each other and swung the pendulums at different rates, they would eventually end up swinging at the same rate.

It has been discovered through modern brain entrainment techniques that when we seek to entrain the brain into a different brainwave state it takes six minutes of entrainment for the brain to be entrained in to a different state.
This is why by minute six the students have slowed down in to an alpha state, letting the stalking shift them in to the

natural brainwave state closer to the Schumann resonance, and then the birds who are one of the most noticeable natural feedback mechanisms of the earth, start to sing, expressing harmony and a zero threat level from the students.

What this means is that if you slow down for six minutes use peripheral vision and walk naturally or even more slowly you will enter an alpha state with very little effort. This in my opinion is the natural state of consciousness of human beings.

The state that is considered the normal state of human consciousness, a faster speed at which the brain can operate, which is called Beta is 13-30hz. (Or cycles per second). For those of us that find it hard to sit still and meditate and struggle to control our physical mind or to be detached from the thought that flow through the mind this practice can silence the physical mind within six minutes or less. So we have already learnt that even before we begin to enter stalking speed by just acting in natural ways like placing our foot with a relaxed ankle and using our peripheral vision our body and mind respond and start to shift into a slower more natural rhythm. A rhythm that as it turns out is closer to the natural frequency of the Earth. This is a very simple yet very profound shift that also creates a resonance of belonging.

ALPHA BREATH DYNAMICS

After many years of working in nature I have developed an intervention called Alpha Breath Dynamics. It has grown out of my understanding of Stalking, Meditation and Martial Arts.

I developed it through studying what occurs while stalking, during meditation and when practicing martial arts and then isolating the components that effectively help one to shift into an Alpha state. This means it is possible to enter an Alpha state faster than the current science suggests with no external intervention i.e. without brain wave entrainment or any external aids.

Having meditated for many years and found how powerfully calming the effects of slowed breathing could be I started to experiment with the stalking movements broken down into segments timed with the breath. While stalking, the breath naturally slows so it seemed to be a natural point of focus. I began working with an in breath of between 4-6 seconds and an out breath of the same length. I have settled on a 5 second in and out breath. I found my state shift seemed to be speeded up by this approach and within two steps i.e. two minutes I felt the shift into the Alpha state.

However trying to coordinate the stalking movements with the breath was quite complicated and moving in slow motion especially standing on one leg has its challenges. I wanted to simplify the process cut away anything unnecessary. So I retained the peripheral vision element from stalking but let go of the attempt different movements taking simple Chi Gung exercise like raising and lowering the hands in coordination with the breath. It was at this point that I realised I was entering an Alpha state within ten to twelve breaths. This is under two minutes. The normal entrainment time through stalking or external methods is about six minutes.

The first test that I ran with this new information was at an event in London. I have a brain wave measuring machine called a mind ball, you put on a head band with sensors in it and if you enter an Alpha state a ball moves along a triangular base to stop in an end zone.

The event was a Buddhist gathering so I thought there would
be experienced meditators present. People tried with mixed
success. Towards the end of the day two teenagers came
over. They had been watching for some time and wanted to
have a go. I let them try and watched them have no success
for about ten minutes, I then suggested they try using
peripheral vision, slowing their breath and synchronising their
hand movements to the breath. Within two minutes they
were having success moving the ball.

This gave me food for thought, had I found a swift way to
help anyone enter the Alpha state and who would this most
benefit?

EXERCISE:

The three components of Alpha breath dynamics are:

1) Full peripheral vision
2) Slowing the breath to 5 seconds in and 5 seconds out.
   (It can be between 4-6 seconds)
3) Synchronising a movement with the breath

My suggestion for your first practice of this is that a
movement is used with the hands outstretched on either side
of the body at the periphery of the vision. Raising the hands
as you breathe in and lowering as you breathe out. This helps
to keep your eyes in peripheral vision as the movement at the
periphery of your vision is noticeable.

This should be practiced for a minimum of two minutes.

Practicing it for longer has additional benefit. I discovered that the Heart Math Institute use the 5 second breathing speed and have researched this for over 20 years. Their focus has been on measuring the sine wave that the heart produces. This is normally somewhat erratic. Their research shows that five minutes of practice of the five second in and out breath produces what they call heart coherence. This is a very even sine wave that the heart is producing; the benefit of this is a quality of inner emotional stability that can last for up to four hours with only five minutes of practice.

My assessment of this is that Alpha is the state of calmness and focus so it is inevitable that if we are slowing the brainwave state a bi-product is a calmer heart. If we run an experiment and isolate the breathing we find that we do not get the Alpha shift, whereas when we do the Alpha breath dynamics we gain both shifts, Heart Coherence and the shift to Alpha.

Once we have mastered the art of using our peripheral vision we can simplify the movement to the raising and lowering of a single finger. What my research has shown is that the movement is unimportant, as long as it is synchronised with the breath. It is also possible to slow down the brain wave state even further and drop in to the Theta range with a few adjustments but this is beyond the scope of this book.

.

2

WORK

To be able to apply theories and experiences of flow to the work place we can start by looking at the current scientific perspective on the flow state. In order to do this we need to look at the work of Mihaly Csikszentmihalyi. Mihaly is known as the originator of positive psychology, a world war two survivor who became interested in the study of happiness after the war. His book Flow was published in 1990 and has been translated in to multiple languages and it has been applied in many fields worldwide.

The pronunciation of his name looks a bit tricky and so here is a simple way to phonetically pronounce his name:

"Me high? Cheeks send me high!"

"I developed a theory of optimal experience based on the concept of flow—the state in which people are so involved in an activity that nothing else seems to matter; the experience itself is so enjoyable that people will do it even at great cost, for the sheer sake of doing it"

– Mihaly Csikszentmihalyi, Flow (page 4)

Mihaly Csikszentmihalyi developed a theory by interviewing many athletes, artists and people working in education (Nakamura & Csikszentmihalyi, 2002) inspiring a direction of study in to finding happiness. His work led him to create a list of eight characteristics of flow.

THE 8 CHARACTERISTICS OF FLOW

Mihaly Csikszentmihalyi describes eight characteristics of flow:

1. Complete concentration on the task;
2. Clarity of goals and reward in mind and immediate feedback;
3. Transformation of time (speeding up/slowing down);
4. The experience is intrinsically rewarding;
5. Effortlessness and ease;
6. There is a balance between challenge and skills;
7. Actions and awareness are merged, losing self-conscious rumination;
8. There is a feeling of control over the task.

I would like firstly to examine these characteristics, because from my own research I have found a number of the characteristics to be slightly contradictory or not strictly necessary.

I also offer my own list that adds to Csikszentmihalyi's which contains a number of characteristics I have found are intrinsic to this state and do not seem to be covered by Csikszentmihalyi's list. His list consists of pointers that help us to reverse engineer the flow state from the characteristics. Most of his characteristics are very useful and I agree with many of them though I would like to contextualise a few of them before offering my additions.

1. Complete concentration on the task;

If accessing the flow state is the task, as in the Alpha breath dynamics, once that is achieved there needs to be no specific task to focus on in order to remain in the flow state.

The assertion that concentration on the task is a characteristic arises because Csikszentmihalyi's research centres on people who are involved in <u>activities</u> that bring them in to the flow state. When accessing the flow state is the *autotelic* activity (i.e. an activity done for the pleasure it gives to the doer) then there is no other task required once the state is achieved.

2. Clarity of goals and reward in mind and immediate feedback;

With the goal setting there are several caveats:

i.   The goals need to be attainable
ii.   This means if there is a process to learn, it needs to be broken down in too easy to accomplish stages. Stages that also mark the progress of the skill development. Giving positive feedback.
iii. Feedback is important and this may be a subjective feeling shift of entering the flow state. Part of the self-rewarding nature of the state shift.
iv.   If the experience is intrinsically rewarding as is stated in characteristic number four then goal setting is in conflict with this characteristic. Unless it is in alignment with the enjoyment of the activity and not at odds with it.

With the characteristics 3-5 I am in total agreement.

3. Transformation of time (speeding up/slowing down);

The feeling of adsorption the first of my characteristics echoes this loss of sense of time. The merging with the task makes us lose track of the passage of time, this is how we can tell we have naturally slipped in to the flow state.

4. The experience is intrinsically rewarding;

The shift in to the flow state is more peaceful internally, less anxious more connected to self, environment and other. So any activity that gives us this respite whether focused or just using the state shift is intrinsically rewarding.

5. Effortlessness and ease;

I would characterise this as a quality of fluidity or stillness as it can be expressed as either but on the whole agree with this characteristic. The calmness the state shift brings can create a resting in stillness. Movement that is not fluid can break the flow both for the self and those in the immediate environment. Similarly the intrusion of thought can break the flow.

6. There is a balance between challenge and skills;

With this characteristic ideas of risk start to enter the picture and yet we have as part of the evidence of accessing flow states reports of Tai chi practitioners experiencing flow, where there is no risk. So we need to be a bit careful in extrapolating the need for risk. It is not essential and where it is part of the challenge skills balance it is a calculated risk. i.e. the person is operating within certain known parameters and increasing the challenge in an incremental way.

This aspect is useful for keeping us motivated while not being necessary if we are experiencing the fourth characteristic of the activity being intrinsically rewarding. So I would list this under characteristics that can increase our focus and maintain motivation, possibly even deepening our flow state. So this is more of a way of advancing our capacity rather than an intrinsic characteristic.

Curiosity on the other hand my second characteristic is in my assessment the main way we remain engaged and move out of boredom and this is about having questions about what is around us and is not linked to challenge, skill or risk.

7. Actions and awareness are merged, losing self-conscious rumination;

I am in total agreement with this one though the loss of self-conscious rumination is very specific, I would broaden this out to say that the Alpha flow state has the capacity to quieten the mind as in my third characteristic, lack of internal dialogue.

8. There is a feeling of control over the task.

With number eight I struggle with the language as for me the access in to the flow state creates more of a quality of surrender to the state or activity. A sense of control implies some part of us is outside the activity, if by control Csikszentmihalyi is meaning there is a sense of certainty that we can accomplish the task, a feeling that we can do it. Then I have no argument.

'What people enjoy is not the sense of *being* in control, but the sense of *exercising* control in difficult situations'

Csikszentmihalyi (1990, p. 61)

Csikszentmihalyi (1993, p. 181) suggested this dimension is more of a 'sense of control' where individuals feel like they are unstoppable or feel like they can achieve anything.

Keller & Blomann (2008) found that the sense of exercising control in difficult situations is central to the flow experience.

This I would characterise as an inner knowing based on previous experience that creates both the capacity to asses 'challenge skill balance' and the 'sense of control' is built on previous success with incremental progress.

8 ADDITIONAL CHARACTERISTICS OF FLOW

1. Adsorption, oneness;
2. Attitude of curiosity, fully present;
3. Lack of internal dialogue;
4. Greater sensory awareness, greater feeling/sensing capacity;
5. Increased intuition and creativity;
6. Lack of anxiety and striving; Playful attitude
7. Increased connection with environment, self and other;
8. Capacity to take in and remember information and circumstances.

Here is a short description of each of the Characteristics:

1. Adsorption, oneness;

The first characteristic is the main quality that is experienced when in the flow state. If a task is being performed then the quality of awareness and action merging is experienced. If no task is taking place and the person is in the flow state then they still feel a quality of adsorption that is usually felt as a sense of increased awareness and presence. This can be felt as a sense of unity with self, activity or environment or all three.

'The loss of the sense of self separate from the world around it is sometimes accompanied by a feeling of union with the environment'

Page 63 Flow

2. Attitude of curiosity, fully present;

Most autotelic activities are generated by curiosity. Curiosity draws the investigator in to what they are curious about and has no defined end point. The lack of end point brings them in to a state of being present. Where awareness is focused through the cognitive function by asking questions it draws the questioner in to a direct relationship with their surroundings. This brings more attention to their senses i.e. movement and sound that is occurring in their vicinity rather than self-criticism or mental description of activity.

3. Lack of internal dialogue;

As well as losing the critical aspect of the internal dialogue that helps to free a person of their self-consciousness, there is also a reduction in all of the internal dialogue. This has a significant impact on anxiety and worry as this dialogue quietens down. If it flares up we are pulled out of the flow state. Worry generally only relates to situations and people that are elsewhere in place or time. So the space that we can get from this internal dialogue that promotes worry can be a primary reason we undertake the practice that produces the flow state. The prefrontal cortex that processes self-critical thought is shut down when in the flow state.

This also contributes to our ability to reach out to others as we are no longer subject to the self-critical elements that can stand in the way of initial communication. When the self-praising aspect appears we are similarly thrown out of the flow state. This is similarly quietened by the flow state as well.

4.   Greater sensory awareness, greater feeling/sensing capacity;

As we shift from the mental chatter that is a major feature of the Beta state our senses begin to open. Our hearing increases, our depth of field goes to infinity and we become hypersensitive to tiny movements. Our night vision increases, and our capacity to feel through the body increases. We become able to locate objects and people and navigate our environment through the feeling sense in the body as well as visually and through hearing.

There is a quality of sensing the field around the body and the ability to access information that can come from this such as sensing a person's trajectory or intention.

5.   Increased intuition and creativity;

As the feeling sense increases we become able to anticipate the movement of the objects and people around us and anticipate how to move ourselves in relation to those outer aspects. We can sense the line or pathway a person or object is about to take. This becomes an intuitive response to the environment. Reading emotion more easily in others and feeling their intentions.

We also become able to respond to stimulus with increased choice, thus creating new and different responses to similar stimuli. This increases our creativity as the tendency is to act with more fluidity both physically, mentally and emotionally.

6. Lack of anxiety and striving; Playful attitude

When we try we tend to fail, we need to 'try softer' not harder; to relax and play rather than to concentrate in a serious manner. Relaxation allows our bodies to move more naturally and therefore to perform better. When in the flow state there is a quality of trust in the body that removes a lot of tension and striving. When the internal dialogue is shut down and our focus is entirely in the present two things occur. We are both taking a break from our self-chatter, which in itself is refreshing and are free of thoughts that are denying our capacity while we try to act. So there is less mental and emotional friction. This is summed up by maintaining a playful attitude. So if we fail we chalk it up to experience and learn from it, we treat 'failure' as feedback. We are investing in loss, when we have made all the mistakes and learned from them we can do it right every time.

7. Increased connection with environment, self and other;

As we start to connect with the environment through the increase in our feeling sense we start to feel a two way connection. We are receiving information from the environment which is not available when we are in a Beta state. As the flow or Alpha state is a similar resonance to the natural earth resonance, our two fields become more aligned allowing a natural information exchange.

This connection with the natural world is a non-judgemental

connection with other living organisms which allows more emotional space for us to connect with ourselves. This happens through connecting with domestic and wild animals as well as plants, trees, rivers and the sea. The unconditional love of a dog, the clear reflection a horse might give and the broader reflection that nature gives. Nature reflects us back to ourselves and can help us to see where we are in ourselves. Once we have re-established a connection with ourselves we can find it easier to connect with others. This is the basis of much nature based therapy.

8. Capacity to take in and remember information and circumstances.

When our experience is very vivid and we are really present we can retain information more easily. When we are relaxed this assists in our capacity for remembering information. When we feel that a subject is second nature it is much easier to adsorb and reiterate the subject.

THE MAP IS NOT THE TERRITORY

The dissection of the flow state that Csikszentmihalyi has skilfully masterminded can help us design environments and ways of working that increase the flow state. Yet Csikszentmihalyi has not developed any direct method of accessing the flow state instead he has tried to map out the characteristics of it. This map is like an outline of a state rather than a direct way of accessing it.

"So how can we reach this elusive goal that cannot be attained by a direct route? My studies of the past quarter-century have convinced me that there is a way. It is a circuitous path that begins with achieving control over the contents of consciousness"

Page 3 Flow

We do know however that 'the map is not the territory'. Reverse engineering ourselves in to the flow state from the outline or characteristics is Csikszentmihalyi's strategy.

However when it is possible to access the territory through a simple natural method that only takes two minutes we can find ourselves in this state without even knowing about the characteristics. Alpha breath dynamics is a way of mastering our consciousness and no intellectual study or 'circuitous path' is required.

If however we combine our personal experience of the flow state through the Alpha breath dynamics and greater intellectual understanding through Csikszentmihalyi's characteristics then we enhance both our theoretical and actual knowledge.

Csikszentmihalyi notes that even if there were an ancient method that our ancestors used to access the flow state there are still reasons that inhibit people from actualising the balance and happiness that can come from such a method. If this were know in the past there is not much evidence of this having been passed down as today we can struggle with ways of accessing happiness.

Csikszentmihalyi goes on to state correctly that any method would not just be a cognitive one but one that includes the emotions. And that if it had been known then whether or not it had been applied would be the real test. The main issue is that it needs to be chosen by the individual and practiced. Control over our own consciousness is a personal choice so cannot be institutionalised. Csikszentmihalyi also states that this mechanism of personal control over consciousness needs to be reinvented for every epoch.

It seems that those who take the trouble to gain mastery over what happens in consciousness do live a happier life.

Page 23

I would like to highlight this point that the choice to practice and then practicing are of extreme importance. Here is an anecdote that helps to illustrate this. I was running a family based camp with around fifty people attending. As an experiment I shared the Alpha breath dynamics with everyone at the start of the camp. I also suggested that they have a go at practicing the technique on their own in the forest to see what happened. A few days later I asked when everyone was gathered if anyone had had a go in the forest. A woman put up her hand and shared how she had wandered off in to the woods and tried and immediately the birds had started to sing around her and a beautiful calm came over her. I looked around the circle and no one else spoke. I reflected to the group that out of fifty participants I had one student.

So there is much to agree with in Csikszentmihalyi findings however there are a number of places where my findings differ. It might seem wildly presumptuous for a non-scientist to be questioning a well-respected theory that has been applied worldwide. Though there are anomalies that Csikszentmihalyi notes himself and certain assumptions on which his theory is based that when we apply parallel theories to, we come to different conclusions.

My motivation is to enhance our journey towards happiness and widen the skilful application of this information.

We may need to look at some anomalies that Csikszentmihalyi himself notes, the redefining of certain interpretations of some of the examples he gives and the specific psychological framework he has chosen to use as his basis for consciousness. There is no denying the immense contribution Csikszentmihalyi has made to this field. The phenomenological model that Csikszentmihalyi chose as his model of consciousness works very well in the context of reported experience, so it is clear why this was chosen as the basis for his exploration. Even so when there are other models of consciousness like the measurement of brainwave states that have been with us since the 1920's and surged in popularity and effectiveness in the 1960's we do need to question why this research has not been woven in to the theories on flow.

ANOMALIES IN THE FLOW MODEL AT WORK

Csikszentmihalyi noted certain anomalies in his research about work and leisure. This was in relation to flow experienced in leisure time and what was characterises as flow with in work;

This anomaly hinges around the challenge skills balance at work. Respondents to Csikszentmihalyi's survey reported a higher challenge skill balance at work than during leisure times this suggests the person is in a higher state of flow if this is a necessary characteristic. The anomaly was that they were also asked if they would rather be somewhere else, and the responses were high at work (that they would rather be somewhere else) and very low whilst engaging in leisure activities.

'Flow' Page 159.

This anomaly, that in leisure time, there is a lower challenge skills balance yet a greater enjoyment and less desire to be elsewhere, points to relaxation and choice being important parts of the flow state. This supports my assertion that the challenge skill balance can enhance the flow state where motivation is needed.

This aspect is useful for keeping us motivated while not being necessary if we are experiencing the fourth characteristic of the activity being intrinsically rewarding. So I would list this under characteristics that can increase our focus and maintain motivation possibly even deepening our flow state. So this is more of a way of advancing our capacity rather than an intrinsic characteristic.

The second characteristic that I list of curiosity is almost in place of the challenge skill balance. There are several places where Csikszentmihalyi interprets the asking of questions, that I link directly to curiosity, as the challenge skills balance.

To me curiosity drives the autotelic personality. That is the engagement in activities for the enjoyment inherent in them. We may be developing or honing a skill which creates a defined focus and it is this calm focus that is allied with the flow state. Or we may be making an inquiry in to our immediate environment that brings us in to the moment.

Csikszentmihalyi examines several accounts of prisoners of war and their strategies of how to maintain mental flow by staying present and using their imagination to remain free.

"Richard Logan, who has studied the accounts of many people in difficult situations, concludes that they survived by finding ways to turn the bleak objective conditions into subjectively controllable experiences. They followed the blueprint of flow activities. First, they paid close attention to the most minute details of their environment, discovering in it hidden opportunities for action that matched what little they were capable of doing,"

Flow Page 90

This notion of paying close attention to detail appears nowhere else in his writings on flow and it's interpretation as a challenge skills balance in this case obscures from us the importance of questioning. In Christopher Burney's quoted account of being a prisoner of war, he muses on the bed he lays in asking question after question about its construction etc.. until he runs out of questions and then starts on something else. This is the exercise of curiosity the second characteristic I put forward, that draws us in to the present with infinity of possible places to become curious.

It is when we sink in to feeling like a victim that our spirit can be broken. Choice is the enemy of the victim. So if we maintain access to infinity of choice through questioning this helps us to maintain resilience as well as presence. This leads me to the conclusion that curiosity and questioning are primary rather than our focus hinging around a challenge skill's balance and seeking feedback.

The other aspect that arises in these accounts is a mental freedom being achieved with the imagination, a kind of focused daydreaming. Either by prisoners imagining playing golf or walking home. This inner freedom keeping the prisoner focused.

Flow Page 91.

What I see as an anomaly of curiosity and questioning

replacing the idea of the challenge skill balance and feedback, comes up in one of the three examples Csikszentmihalyi uses to illustrate autotelic workers.

Joe from Chicago who had been fascinated with machinery since being a child and was the lynch pin of the company he worked for. Not wanting to be promoted but happy to work the production line welding train cars, able to jump in and do any of the production line jobs with ease and joy. He was also able to fix any machine from a giant crane to a toaster. He was as busy in his spare time creating a watering system that produced rainbows at the touch of a button. This is what he said that as a kid…

"Like when my mother's toaster went on the fritz, I asked myself: 'If I were that toaster and I didn't work, what would be wrong with me?'"

Flow Page 148

This illustrates that what his interest rests on is this fantastic question:

'If I were that toaster and I didn't work, what would be wrong with me?'

It is the question that drives him. That engages him with the object it is not a sense of challenge.

Exercise eight below is an invitation to start asking questions to build curiosity and this excellent question can be adapted to anything that is not working within or around us.

WELL-BEING AND THE FLOW STATE

The flow state has great implications for well-being an important focus for those in the workplace. As we see stress and boredom causing disengagement, lack of productivity and leading to illness. Using the characteristics of flow with the Alpha breath dynamics we can create ways to keep ourselves or our employees engaged, increasing resilience and creativity.

With an increased focus on wellbeing in nature, it is becoming clear that by just being in the forest or a natural environment people can access the calm and focused Alpha state. This is because natures resonance; known as the Schuman resonance, is resonant at the lower levels of Alpha.

We experience a relief from the incessant voice of the prefrontal cortex which is where the self-critical activity comes from and is active in the beta state. In Alpha this internal dialogue can and does shut down, allowing more clarity and presence, this often being the main driver for people enjoying the flow state. This is the natural state for humans but not the state that is considered normal, which is the faster Beta state.

According to Arne Dietrich, the flow state has been associated with decreased activity in the prefrontal cortex (2003).

The prefrontal cortex is an area of the brain responsible for higher cognitive functions such as self-reflective consciousness, memory, temporal integration, and working memory. It's an area that's responsible for our conscious and explicit state of mind.

However, in a state of flow, this area is believed to temporarily down-regulate in a process called transient hypofrontality. This temporary inactivation of the prefrontal area may trigger the feelings of distortion of time, loss of self-consciousness, and loss of inner critic.

Just by simply leaving the office and spending time in a more natural environment with our colleagues' tensions can be eased and conflicts can resolve.

"I have worked with corporate clients for many years and have witnessed how often the most potent moments of change and progress come while sat around the fire after a day in the outdoors."

Pete Jones, The Soul Camp.

With the Alpha breath dynamics we can bring this forest state of mind with us wherever we go. We become generators of this frequency able to quieten the internal dialogue, and feel calm and focused, thus reducing several of the main causes of stress.

Stress tends to shut down our capacity to access our internal resources, thus reducing our capacity to think creatively. When we relax in to the flow state we can access greater levels of creativity. This can help us find more effective solutions to whatever the problems we are facing and can help us adapt more readily to change one of the main components of personal and business resilience.

At a personal level when we are in a more creative frame of mind we can come up with many more choices as to how we respond to inner and outer stimulus. This helps to combat stressful experience which can causes a diminishment of choice, perhaps even reducing our choice down to the level of our trauma response; fight, flight, freeze and collapse. So by expanding our creative state which increases our capacity to come up with more choices and at the same time remaining calm we increase our ability to respond skilfully rather than react to people and situations.

When we feel disempowered and in a state of the diminishment of choice this can be called the place of the 'victim'. We tend to behave defensively and take less personal responsibility for what is going on. We can freeze in negotiations or make mistakes, or get angry with our co-workers. We know we are experiencing the victim state when we hear ourselves say, 'I had no choice'.

This means that choice is the enemy of victimhood and creativity is the generator of choice.

When we stay curious in relation to the situation or person and are specifically curious about what appears to be the problem we tend to uncover many more choices. Then we can exit the victim state and feel more present and empowered to act.

Csikszentmihalyi noted that one of the main complaints workers sited was conflict with other people in the work place.

Recently a colleague of mine was finding it difficult because those who were supposed to be supporting her were continuously raising problems. Being aware of issues and problems is important and I made a few suggestions to illustrate several possible choices that could help:

1) Ask your support staff to bring solutions rather than problems i.e. encourage them to flag up the issues and come with several possible ways to deal with it. In this process they might already sort out the issues before it gets to you and it creates a good habit of engagement with problems in them.

2) A second suggestion I made was, that if someone spots a problem they should be encouraged to be the one to take responsibility for dealing with it.

3) Thirdly, if something some one feels something is missing then invite them to bring what they want to find i.e. create the culture you would like to be a part of.

Changing our state so that we can increases inner choice, combined with curiosity towards whatever we perceive to be the obstacle, builds personal resilience. When we treat each situation as an interesting puzzle to solve rather than a personal affront or insurmountable obstacle we are in a better position to manage both our internal experience and the external situation.

When this is supported by two other characteristics:

1) The discipline of not taking anything personally.

2) Considering everything to be interesting rather than good or bad.

Resilience is vastly increased as we conserve a lot of emotional energy that would otherwise be used up in reaction to taking things personally or getting caught up in the unfolding drama of labelling things as good or bad.

Not taking things personally is a choice. It demands a considerable amount of self-awareness and self-discipline. We need to be skilful enough in our communication to know that we are not unduly causing reactions in others. This happens when we are expressing our needs and inner experience with emotional sovereignty and kindness.

(See: emotional sovereignty and Good and Bad, in the chapter on Love)

Fritz & Avsec (2007) examined the connection between music student's propensity to experience flow and there subjective experience of well-being. What they found was when flow states are experienced this is a good predictor of a person's capacity to experience a feeling of well-being. Myers & Diener, (1995) had also previously made this link. This should not really be a surprise as flow sates in themselves promote wellbeing.

So when there is a culture that encourages Alpha states within a company by introducing practices that increase access to the Alpha state during working hours. Like practicing the Alpha breath dynamics, combined with activities that are structured so that they intrinsically increase flow, we can accomplish multiple positive outcomes; Increased creativity, personal resilience and wellbeing. This translates to greater adaptability and business resilience with a healthier and more responsive workforce.

So there are now two approaches we can combine to increase flow, the development of inner resources for those undertaking the work, to increase personal access to the Alpha state. While structuring the work so it increases flow by bringing in Csikszentmihalyi's characteristics in to play.

'The more a job inherently resembles a game-with variety, appropriate and flexible challenges, clear goals, and immediate feedback-the more enjoyable it will be regardless of the workers level of development.'

Flow Page 152

MOTIVATION, CREATIVITY AND FLOW

Fullagar & Mills (2008) found that flow and motivation are linked, finding that people experiencing a high level of motivation also experience high flow levels. If you think about the excitement that certain prospects can elicit, a child waking up at four in the morning at Christmas, or getting up early to catch a flight to go on holiday. Where there is the prospect of excitement and joy linked to work then there will be motivation. So engaging in work that we love is the greatest motivation. If this is not possible all the time then we can gain satisfaction from the accomplishment of a task by ticking it off our list.

When we can break down tasks in to manageable pieces and set attainable goals we increase engagement and motivation. This allows us to focus on one piece at a time which increases our ability to access the flow state. As we can then be giving each piece our undivided attention. As our capacity with the flow state increases we become more able to flow with multiple tasks.

Andrew Huberman asserts that it is possible to increase this capacity and sustain our ability to maintain flow for longer using a simple practice. That is to acknowledge to ourselves each time we reach a goal.

We can break down our day in to acknowledgement points 'Wow I made it to coffee break' or break down a task in to small segments. Like 'Wow I just wrote another paragraph'. Run some experiments to verify this.

EXERCISE:

Find a task or process and decide on certain time points or achievement points. When you reach each stage acknowledge to yourself your accomplishment. Does this enhance your flow state?

The one I chose to run when I first heard this as I was driving was to acknowledge to myself each time I passed a particular land mark. My drive home was about 20 minutes and I created an acknowledgement landmark every 5 minutes. I arrived home feeling more awake and refreshed. It works well if you have a daily list and you self-acknowledge each task you tick off the list.

There are some tasks that require the flow state to be accomplished well. Any artistic or creative task is enhanced by the flow state and similarly can be a way in to this state. This means we can find ourselves in a catch 22 situation. We have half an hour in our busy schedule in which to enter the timeless state of flow in order to come up with the right idea for a brief, presentation, logo design, report etc. These are complex tasks often with multiple stages and we may be interrupted either by a chance phone call or a scheduled meeting. When we break the task down in to sections that we know can be accomplished in the half an hour we have. We can access the flow state and both enhance our capacity to accomplish the task and enjoy the process of being in the flow state while we do it.

I applied this to my fine art painting process, which for years I could only engage with if I was in 'the mood'. Not realising that the mood was the flow state. Then when I had children it seemed impossible to both be in the mood and have enough time to be able to paint a picture. So I broke it down in to a series of stages:

1. Taking photos and or sketching.
2. Printing the images for me to be able to select the starting point.

3. Preparing the board or canvas.
4. Priming the board or canvas.
5. Laying down the base colours for the painting.
6. Finally making the painting.

Each stage could be done in short bursts, yet I had always felt this to be one continuous process that had to be done in the flow of a day or two when I was in the right mood.

I am using this as an example as the creative process is much more vulnerable to being inhibited by interruption than work based tasks we might have on our to do list. Yet it is possible to break them down and be fully engaged in the flow state whilst completing each stage. This may also seem like common sense, yet it took me a while to implement this strategy and this was before I had developed the Alpha breath dynamics technique.

EXERCISE:

Choose a complex task you want or need to be doing multiple times. It could be something you have always wanted to be able to do under your current circumstances or something you have to do whilst being continuously interrupted by work or domestic interruptions. Break it down in to easily manageable steps of half an hour. It could be less time if you are interrupted more frequently. Start with the first part of the task, go through the Alpha breath dynamics for two minutes then engage fully with the task. Knowing you may be interrupted but that you are just focussed on that one part of the job or task. This way you can be totally adsorbed in the task for this set amount of time.

There is no surprise that by creating enjoyment; motivation and concentration can follow, together these aspects can create a feeling of flow within the individual (Bonaiuto, Mao,

Roberts, Psalti, Ariccio, Ganucci Cancellieri, & Csikszentmihalyi, 2016).

So the more we can make our work enjoyable the more motivation and concentration accompanies our joy. One way that we can structure our day if we are not feeling motivated is to bounce between tasks that we enjoy and ones that we don't. We can use the energy of enjoyable tasks or the promise of them to motivate us to work through the difficult and mundane tasks we have to do. Remembering to harness the feeling of accomplishment that we can get from the completion of mundane tasks, by savouring this feeling once we have completed such a task. Focusing on this can help us enjoy the work and can add to our motivation.

CURIOSITY AND LEARNING FOR ITS OWN SAKE

If you are reading this book then it is more than likely that you are an *autotelic* personality. Someone who does things for their own sake, *autotelic* activities are some of the most rewarding. Perhaps you have chosen activities to learn and practice that take a while to develop competence. Activities that it is hard to say you have mastered hence there is always a quality of learning associated with the activity even when you reach a high level. This could be through physical activities like martial arts, golf, rock climbing or artistic endeavours like learning to play music, taking up cabinet making or painting or perhaps they are more intellectual like learning a new language or solving increasingly difficult puzzles.

This characteristic is linked to curiosity or rather is powered by it. When we were children we were curious to the point of annoying our parents and all of those around us. Then at some point we lost this interest, this inquiry in to the world we live in. If this is not our modus operandi how do we reengage this characteristic? It increases our experience of engagement with the world around us and our experience of flow. This can be a force that helps to direct our working life, whether we are an artist, scientist or we are in business. Asking good questions helps us explore interesting dramatic dilemmas as a playwright. As a scientist we might be re-examining things that were considered constant or wanting to find out how to treat a particular disease. In business we can gain an advantage by being curious about new approaches either within an organisation or how it is delivered or presented to the market.

WHAT IS A GOOD QUESTION AND SO IS HOW

In his book 'Never split the difference' Chris Voss an ex F.B.I. chief hostage negotiator talks about open ended calibrated questions, and their effect on others. When faced with the demand for money in order to return a hostage his first go to question is:

'How am I supposed to do that?'

This shifts the onus on to the kidnapper to find the solution and allows the negotiator more time and the possibility to gather more information about who they are dealing with.

Or 'How do I know they are still alive?'

This is a major step in any hostage negotiation, getting a proof of life and this way of asking means there is no obligation to offer something in return. The request for help creates a collaborative feeling in the kidnapper.

What possible reason could there be to suddenly start talking about hostage negotiations? You may well ask. Well with a hostage negotiation one has to make sure the theory is built proof. This digression is to point out the power of skilful questions. Another question that I use in many difficult relationship situations is:

'What do you need?' or 'is there something you need?'

Then allowing space for the other to express whatever it is they really need, this might just be reassurance or a hug.

This can then be followed by "do you need a hug?" or what might feel appropriate to offer. Rather than blocking, contradicting or reacting to their state or point of view.

I also use this question when confronted by a stranger acting in a violent way, for several reasons:

The first is that when we are thinking we are generally not acting. So this encourages a slowing down and change of modality.

Secondly this question usually needs to be answered through knowing what we are feeling so the modality shift can bring the person in to contact with the emotion behind their action.

Thirdly this then starts to encourage them to feel what would help them rather than their expression of pain through aggression.

I have been in an extreme situation where I have used this more as a statement rather than a question. I was at a small weekend outdoor family event with less than five hundred people. I was teaching and running workshops there. There was a café set up nearby and one afternoon the café proprietor kicked off and was making a huge disturbance as he railed at the top of his voice inside his café marquee. I saw parents grabbing their children's hands as they disappeared from the scene.

I on the other hand a martial artist of many years and through that training a peacemaker, thought 'Oh dear one of my brothers is upset I had better go and see what the problem is' I entered the tent and the café owner continued his furious rant. I saw his best friend crouched down on the opposite side of the counter trying to logically talk him down. These were all good strategies I thought, making yourself smaller and less threatening, putting the counter between you and who you are negotiating with and talking sense. But we were passed any of these being useful. We were passed any point where rationality would help. I had entered with no strategy and as I stood in the door way, a statement came out. I summoned the same power of communication he was using and shouted with full force....

'YOU NEED A HUG!!!'

He stopped shouting and slowly a look of confusion came over his face, he then softly said 'huh??.... Yes I do'. I then went over and hugged him and the whole situation deescalated. On reflection I see that this emotional matching and pacing made it possible for him to hear me. I had only offered him what I felt he needed. Once he reflected on it he agreed.

When people are upset, in a trauma response or in reaction the same questions can really help to bring them back to themselves. These same questions can also help us skilfully negotiate a good deal at work or the return of a hostage. They can also help us engage our curiosity increasing our capacity for autotelic activities.

KNOWING STOPS US FLOWING

How is all this going to help me ask good questions to inspire curiosity?

I have often brought groups of school children in to my woods to teach them about nature connection. Perhaps we pass a bush and they ask;

'What plant is that?'

If I tell them what it is called straight away they will totally lose interest and move on. If I make an inquiry in to the plant by asking them questions like:

'Look at the spikes on that'

'What is the bush using those spikes for?'

'If they are for protection what are they protecting?'

'Do you think those yellow flowers are good to eat?'

'What do they smell of?'

'What do they taste like?'

'What other use could we put the spikes to?'

And so on, the minute I say the bush is called Gorse they think they know it. This stops the inquiry dead. Naming things in this way stops the flow of our investigation. So the skill of staying in the flow that the autotelic activity points to is not getting to the end just going up another level. Knowing can be like a rut that we get in to that stops us from having a fresh experience of the place, people or things around us. If we can get in to a state of unknowing something we can explore it afresh. We can break out of our ruts. I know the bush is called Gorse; that the flowers are edible; that it can be used in various culinary ways that; it has certain medicinal properties. This is common knowledge. Can I get in to a state of unknowing in order to discover things that I can only discover through my personal interaction with the plant?

When I have been in that state I have found I can use the spikes as survival tooth picks. How there is always some part of the bush that is dry and how well it ignites in order to start a fire with the addition of a little birch bark. This information is not in any books or wasn't until now. We become wisest when we enter a state of knowing nothing like Plato said:

"I am the wisest man alive, for I know one thing, and that is that I know nothing."

(When asked how he came to this conclusion, he replies my wife told me. I don't think this is historically accurate but I found it amusing)

This is a difficult attitude to take when we are holding a position of responsibility, to enter a place of not knowing, as it can give us a fresh perspective. There are various tricks that artists use when they are struggling to see what might not be right with their painting. Such as turning it upside down or looking at it via a mirror. We can find ways to unknow our work environment in order to get a view of what is not working.

Please take care when you try some of these exercises. You might want to try it with a colleague so you can care take each other during the exercise.

Exercise 1: Breaking your ruts. We are used to taking the

same route to work every day. Choose to come to work a different way. If that is not possible make sure you notice something that you have never noticed before along the same route.

Exercise 2: Reverse perspective. Walk backwards through your work space or if you can to your work space.

Exercise 3: Narrow the aperture. Wear a blindfold or close your eyes when listening to someone or moving through your 'known' environment. You can also wear ear defenders with eyes open and try the same.

Exercise 4: Gain another perspective. Have one of your co-workers/ employees describe the working environment or a job or project to you in a voice or video recording.

Exercise 4.A: Have one of your co-workers/ employees move through the work space videoing and describing it.

Exercise 5: Turn the job upside down. Have the employees be boss for 10 minutes/hour/ day. (Hard to pull off if you are self-employed.) Or use some kind of role play that helps every one experience their job from a different vantage point.

Exercise 6: Addressing blind spots in the chain of command. Task a co-worker preferably a subordinate to criticise what you are doing once a week/ month. The criticism needs to be scheduled for a defined period of time like half an hour once a fortnight. This is so it is contained and there needs to be no come back on them.

Exercise 7: Reverse engineer your solution: Decide where you want to be in work terms, this could be a project or a promotion and figure the path there from the end point to where you are now.

Exercise 8: Stimulating curiosity: In your work environment when you have a spare moment formulate as many questions as you can about your direct environment. What is the reason the desks are organised in this way? Which compass direction am I facing? Does that affect the quality of my work?

Then apply this questioning process to each member of staff you are working with: what is their specific role in this project? Do they have the necessary skill set? How are they feeling about the project?

Then to a specific project: How can I use all my experience to make this project really work? Where have I failed in the past with this type of project and how can I overcome the difficulties I experienced before? What are my blind spots? How am I feeling about the project? How can I increase my level of excitement about this project?

When things aren't working: You could try; if I were that presentation and I didn't work, what would be wrong with me? If I were that project and I was going of track, how would I get back on track?

Here are just a few ideas that wake us up to our ruts and then start to use the resources around us to help us move forwards. Each exercise creates a fresh perspective by creating unknowing in a known environment or breaks a rut.

THE POSATIVE ASPECT OF NAMING THE NEGATIVE

Understanding that naming things solidifies them in the mind almost creating a full stop for what we are talking about is a powerful understanding. We see that it stops the flow of inquiry yet that can work in our favour too.

Voss talks about naming the negative aspects in a negotiation in order to take the sting out of them. He calls it an accusation audit. By empathising with the person you are negotiating with and feeling the negative emotions they could feel on hearing the offer, we anchor their emotion through our opening statement that lists their possible objections.

I consider that by naming the negative emotions we put a full stop after it like when we name something we are inquiring in to. It is then experienced as a known quantity to both parties. Voss then goes on to trigger their aversion to loss which is generally stronger in people than their prospect of gain.

'I got a lousy proposition for you,' I said and paused until each asked me to go on, 'By the time we get off the phone you're going to think I'm a lousy businessman. You're going to think I can't budget or plan. You're going to think Chris Voss is a big talker. His first big project out of the F.B.I. he screws it up completely. He doesn't know how to run an operation. And he might have even lied to me'

And then once I'd anchored their emotions in a minefield of low expectations, I played on their loss aversion.

"Still, I wanted to bring this opportunity to you before I took it to someone else"

P 129 Never split the difference Chris Voss.

So when we think we know something we consider it not worthy of further investigation. Blocking our curiosity and putting a full stop after it thus interrupting the flow. Perhaps we have been doing a business task in a particular way for years and by re-examining it a fresh and implementing a change we could generate a great deal more business. There are points where naming things is a really useful tool to create empathy and take discussion of it off the table. The beauty is that at any point we can reopen that flow by generating a state of unknowing.

SPEEDING UP TIME

When we are in a flow state our perception of time changes, so by just entering a flow state at work we will find the time slips by much more easily. Your time spent will also be more productive as you will be adsorbed in the tasks. Creating manageable steps to accomplish them and taking a moment to acknowledge the accomplishment of each step to extend your flow state.

Intuition and creativity are also heightened so we become able to come at mundane tasks and create enjoyable ways to tackle them, and come up with useful solutions to tricky problems. (Pearce & Conger, 2003) found the flow state expands creativity and allow new ways of thinking about problems.

MINDFULLNESS

We can also bring our full attention on to tasks that we would otherwise be bored by using a quality of adsorption or mindfulness to help us flow with the task.

'A task worth doing is worth doing in a flow state'

We can also be training something quite different when we engage in a mundane task, like in the film 'The karate kid' the young student was being trained in all the basic techniques of karate without realising it; by cleaning cars, sanding floors and painting a fence. He was instructed to do each of these activities in a particular way that developed a certain blocking movement.

So can we take this principle and apply it to the activities we have to do, to make them more enjoyable and flow more easily. We could be mindful of our posture while working, whether sitting at desk or while stacking shelves. We could remember to remain grounded while we move about the office or when talking to others or in a meeting. This could be physical or emotional grounding. Remaining emotionally grounded or centred is based on knowing what we are feeling in the moment and being able to articulate it.

Often in the work place we are not very emotionally centred as we have negotiated a contract in exchange for our time and may have possibly given up some of our natural boundaries in order to secure the contract.

Create challenge

Csikszentmihalyi noted that workers main complaints were:

1. A lack of variety and challenge.
2. Conflict with other people.
3. Stress.

Page 161 Flow

A LACK OF VARIETY AND CHALLENGE

This lack of variety and challenge can be tackled in two different ways. Firstly, by an internal change; the way the worker's attitude can be focused on the job. I have already suggested several approaches to this and secondly by a change of the circumstances of the job. When we reorganise our workplace or job structure to create a state of flow in the person completing the task we will get better results and a happier workforce. This means any way we can gamify the tasks, or increase the number of points of positive acknowledgement we increase flow.

If it is not possible to redesign the workspace or job then adjusting our attitude when we have a mundane task to accomplish may be required in order to overcome the drudgery of the task.

This could be done by the way we in which we stack the shelves or dig the hole, being more mindful of how we are using our body, practicing a Zen like awareness of our surroundings and attention to detail.

I ran a festival for ten years and there was a continuous requirement to be in a state of flow. The range of issues that needed dealing with from distressed people arriving with diverse needs, to artists or caterers not turning up even other co-organisers causing mayhem. There certainly was never a shortage of variety and challenge. This required me to continuously be in a flow state to manage without becoming burned out or having a breakdown. I viewed it as a test of my meditation capacity, if I could move through all the dynamics without losing my temper my meditation was good.

So be careful what you wish for, be prepared to remain in a flow state when you finally get your job with variety and challenge.

CONFLICT WITH OTHER PEOPLE

I have already covered some approaches to dealing with conflict with other people to refresh:

By accessing an Alpha state we remain calm and focused, so our emotional state is more even.

When in Alpha we are more creative and can direct our curiosity towards the problem, removing feelings of victimhood by creating more choices.

If we then bring a curious and experimental attitude to trialling our solutions remembering that the outcome will give us feedback that can then help us adjust our strategy.

Seeing the outcome as feedback helps us move away from thinking we have failed. And if we learn from the feedback it is learning not failure. Without 'failure' creativity and flow are reduced.

STRESS

The Alpha Breath Dynamics already go a long way to reducing stress internally, combine this with skilful ways to work with colleagues and we are well on our way to dealing with this invisible force that can cause so much harm.

Here are two other approaches that can help reduce stress:

TURNING CONFLICT IN TO CONNECTION

When we understand that people in pain do painful things we have the key to turning conflict in to connection. Our normal response to aggression or other negative emotions is to become defensive. If instead we don't take what is being communicated personally we are able to inquire in to the need that is behind the aggressive behaviour. We can ask 'what do you need?' which has a cascading effect as described previously that deescalates the situation and allows us to find out what was driving their aggression. At this point we can then seek to turn the conflict in to connection. In martial arts terms we are yielding in order to advance.

WORK SMART NOT HARD

When we take this adage to heart we can find ourselves with much more time on our hands, time in which to unwind or engage in other pursuits that reduce our stress levels. We might invest several weeks in creating a course that can run remotely generating income for us without further input. Or set up a print on demand inventory free product or shop. Once our enterprise is generating some revenue we can often run these businesses from home or become a digital nomad spending more time with our children or engaged in travel or our hobbies. Tim Ferris's book the four hour work week lays out many useful ways to set up and run businesses remotely.

There is a whole section on working from home in the job you are already in. How to convince your boss you can do those tasks remotely. Since the pandemic we have all shifted our workplace to home taking advantage of the technology that makes this possible. We are uniquely poised to maintain a mixture of this type of work from home and work in the office balance.

3

LOVE

LOVE STORY

Let me tell you a story of a prince and a princess and happily ever after, sound familiar?

We are fed stories of relationship from a very early age and at an early age we form attachments and patterns that can govern us for our whole lives. Whether we are carrying trauma or not is not a question, getting through childhood without experiencing trauma is not really possible. This is not a fatalistic view. We are small sensitive beings and if our parents give us their time and love but they don't have the money for us to have all the things that we want we can suffer. On the other hand we might get everything we desire but none of their time and attention. Even if we get a balance of love and our desires being met, when we step outside the family home we can encounter all sorts of other perspectives that can create trauma.

When we examine who we are attracted to we find that these early traumas can be the imprint we follow. As the other person we are attracted to can carry the exact traits that will recreate our early traumas and thus feels like the home we seek that is embedded in our cellular memory.

This means that when our attraction comes in to play we have an opportunity to explore it before we jump in to a connection. What helps us overcome this, like most obstacles, is awareness of what is in play. When we undo our birth and childhood trauma and skilfully develop a connection with our inner child we can avoid these pitfalls. There is not the scope here to go in to the processes involved in this transformation. Yet our observation of ourselves offers the clues to follow like breadcrumbs. As whatever we have not dealt with from the past is still very much alive in our present it is just under the surface in our unconscious. It gets triggered by others and brought to the surface as the experience of difficult feelings for us to look at.

If this inner child is not consciously integrated it will be unconsciously running the show. By throwing tantrums, building up anger and resentment because we are unable to express ourselves, or other such antics. Our reactions are governed by this part of ourselves, so to achieve any self-mastery we need to develop a skilful relationship to this part of the self.

This chapter is getting a little gloomy as it is examining some of the pitfalls that we can experience as we enter in to relationship. How we navigate these inner feelings affects how skilfully we relate to others.

I wanted to add in here before we continue to look at other issues, some of the benefits of using the Alpha state or flow state in our relationships.

When we shift in to the flow state we become more present,

more embodied and more connected to our feeling sense.

This has a range of benefits, such as when we are more present we can be really attentive and listen with full attention to the other.

We feel more in our bodies and less like the lights are on but nobody is home. This dissociative quality that can inhibit our capacity to communicate in many ways can be overcome by the flow state.

In the Alpha or flow state we are more connected to our senses including our feelings, less in the critical mind, so more able to feel our feelings and then express them more easily.

The difficulty we can have in feelings our feelings often comes from being in a stressed or trauma state. When we are stressed we do not want to connect with our feelings as we are moving towards an adrenalized and reactionary state. This is not conducive to being intimate or self-connected, as we are in the process of shutting down in the face of what seems like a life threatening situation. This can lead to acting out an extreme reaction.

In the beta state the critical mind is very active and so we engage in self-criticism, Judgement, comparisons and expectations. All of these can be quietened down in the flow or Alpha state. What we have been led to believe is that we can only access the flow state in peak athletic experience or through meeting extreme inner boundaries, or flowing with others when we play music. The personal research I have undertaken shows that none of this is essential to accessing these states. We don't even need to engage in some esoteric meditation or Tai-chi practice. We can simply access the flow state through the alpha breath dynamics and then make use of the benefits that the state brings.

PROJECTIONS/ EXPECTATIONS

When we meet another person and are attracted to them there are other dynamics at play as well. We can project on to them all kinds of beauty and power. Often these are our inner qualities that we think we are seeing in the other. These projections attach to the shiny persona we show each other when we first meet. We can be seeing the best version of them and similarly try to project the best version of ourselves. We can also look at the other and see their potential rather than how they are. This can cause all kinds of future conflict as we try to change them rather than get to know them.

We tend to keep all kinds of things hidden that we are ashamed of in ourselves. Difficult dynamics we have experienced in the past and perhaps we are still carrying. Not to mention unconscious behaviour that can be damaging, that we are not even aware of. Because we do not want to be fully seen, out of fear we can put a great effort in to hiding parts of ourselves. Parts we have not accepted in ourselves yet. This can bring up a lot of anxiety that inhibits us being relaxed and present. Alpha breath dynamics can help us calm the anxiety and function more naturally. It might even slow us down enough to help us name these anxieties and bring them in to the open to be let go of.

Projections come from not taking the time to see the whole person, not making a delicate and careful enquiry in to who they are. This is often overridden by our desire our passion or what we call love. The projections translate in to expectations and when we have expectations we are going to cause ourselves suffering.

So here we are attracted to someone who is going to press all the right buttons to bring our trauma to the surface. While we project on to them all these wonderful qualities and possibilities that turn in to expectations. When they don't live up to them we will feel totally justified in being deeply disappointed and upset with them. Of course what we don't realise is that this is happening in both directions. As we mirror each other. So imagine this times two. Is this ever going to work? On top of this emotional balancing act there are the pressures of both people working and possibly having a family. Then there is the lack of support and isolation we can feel with our inner process as our society becomes more and more atomised.

EXPECTATION EXERCISE

Here is an experiment to run: watch just one expectation in you. Watch what happens when it is not met. See how it can turn into a story of suffering that you tell yourself. This story will then justify the feelings that arise when your expectation is not met.

By consciously choosing to pay attention to this process you can understand this mechanism that is in play. The more experiments you run the more you will understand this process and when you understand it fully you will be free of it.

When we have no expectations we have everything.

COMPARISONS

If we also weave in to this mix of projection and expectation how we love to compare ourselves with others. We can up the suffering stakes creating more ways of suffering by comparison. We are all aware of how social media plays a role in this. We are now able to control the narrative of our lives so that things can appear amazing to everyone else when our experience can be awful. Perhaps the amazing relationship we are tweeting and posting everywhere is unfulfilling and limiting. Even before social media this has been an age old game of putting on a good front. We might drive a particular car in order to give the impression that we are doing better than we are or wear fancy suits. When we make comparisons with these projections and ideas we feel that we are not worthy. That we are somehow failing, when five minutes before when we were focused on our job or connecting with our partner we felt fine. Comparing our self with others will only create suffering for us.

COMPARISON EXERCISE

Here is an experiment to run: consciously make a comparison between yourself and another and see how it affects you.

Fill in the blanks:

Their house/car/relationship/ job/ shoes/...........

Is so much: better……../ worse……… than mine.

What do you notice? Could it be that the same thing occurs; that we have made up a story that justifies our emotional response?

EMOTIONAL SOVEREIGNTY

When we are triggered it is someone showing us something we have not dealt yet within our own system. In the cascade of emotion and story that we experience we lose sight of our emotional sovereignty. If we have felt something before, i.e. we have an emotional reference point then it usually has nothing to do with the person or event that triggered it. Though we are apt to shoot the messenger, blaming our partner for what we are experiencing. When we start to take responsibility for what we are feeling and regain our emotional sovereignty we start to create safety in the communication of our emotions.

When we are feeling upset the main thing we need is to be heard. When we feel received often the emotion dissolves.

If it is blocked, by defensiveness, or someone is trying to fix us (when we are not broken only feeling something) or we are silenced when the other is being triggered or worse shamed because they have not dealt with the feeling we are sharing. Or it provokes a reactive emotion like anger when we are being shut down for expressing. All of these responses do not allow us to release the emotional charge that has built up. Therefore it just gets stronger and can fuel a state of anger in us. This is just because we are not being received. How much difficulty in relationship can be dealt with just by listening to the other without judgement or reaction? When we are expressing our feelings without owning them the other feels accused and blamed. If our objective is to be heard then by owning our feelings we make it safe to express even extreme emotional energies. These energies can be very powerful so expressing them safely is a matter of care for the other. We may be expressing "our truth" yet how skilfully we do that is another matter. We can use our idea of "the truth" as a weapon to attack the other or as a way of creating peace.

We can create safety through emotional sovereignty, taking full responsibility for what we are feeling. We need to be paying a great deal of attention to ourselves to see this clearly. We can go for years without understanding this. It takes some time in our own company or some time in isolation to see that the same things trigger us that we would normally blame on someone else. With this understanding we start to experience how we are responsible for our own feelings; both our own happiness and our more difficult feelings. When we know this we no longer put others in charge of our happiness, which is also a great cause of suffering for us and a reason to blame them. This plays out through the language we use, when we say 'I am feeling...' rather than 'You make me feel...' Or 'I am feeling really angry, but not at you.'

If we are with someone who is finding it difficult to be responsible for their feelings we can help by not taking personally what is being shared. As the receiver this can bring safety as we can hear and hold the other without reaction. We are then creating the conditions to be safely heard, which is the main thing we need.

DEFENCE IS A FORM OF ATTACK

I understood very late in life the impact of being defensive. I had trained for years in martial arts and did not realise the somatic impact of the physical form I was practicing. This flowed in to my emotional responses and I was very defensive. Only when I began to practice a really soft martial art called Le Ho Ba fa (Water form) did this change. The main principle of water form is yielding, in order to advance, much as water does when you punch it. It changed me somatically and as I followed the principles not just in the physical practice but also in my emotional life. Through this I become aware of how being defensive is a form of attack and was very painful for my partner.

I also discovered that trying to be right all the time meant that I was making someone else wrong. This seemed to stem from my own insecurity and was a way of raising my feeling of low self-esteem above someone else in order to feel better. My feeling of superiority separated me from others and stemmed from feeling special. After examining this part of myself for some time I decided I was ordinary, extra ordinary. This levelled the playing field removing the feeling of being above or below anyone else creating more self-acceptance and the acceptance of others. This slight change has made it feel like I am alongside those I meet. This has made it possible for me to communicate with anyone no matter their back ground or life experience.

I once apologised to a long time previous partner for always wanting to be right, her humorous response was "That's because you never were" which made me laugh a lot. Who knows she may have meant it.

Letting go of this was a huge relief as we are then exploring together what is going on and there is no fixed point of view that is more correct than any other. For example one of the many points of friction that can arise in relationships is the clash between a logical view of events and an emotional view. 'Well this is what happened…' 'But this is what I felt'

Many times I made the other wrong for feeling, with my own account of events, when feeling is its own modality. Logic and emotions are like two different languages that it is difficult to translate between.

Feelings that arise from the time in our childhood before we could speak are very difficult to articulate. Because of this when we are in a feeling mode it can be hard to think or put words around the feeling. Giving time to each other for this process is crucial again in creating safety of expression.

Our emotional speeds can be very different and even though we could generalise and say that men's emotional speed is slower this is not necessarily always the case. I felt for a long time that when asked how I felt in a tricky situation it was like lowering a bucket in to my well of feelings it needed to be lowered down and then collect the feeling in the bucket and then be brought back to the surface for me to examine. If this process was interrupted at any point the bucket would fall back down in to the well and I would have to start the process all over again. Without having uncovered what I was feeling.

It was only through learning P.E.T. parent effectiveness training that I realised the importance of knowing what I was feeling in the moment. As what is suggested in this training is that we use a three part I message:

'I am feeling … because of this specific behaviour …..and it will have this effect…' these are the three parts of the 'I message'. The feeling we are having, the behaviour that triggered the feeling and the result. We are taking responsibility for the feeling, though before we can do this we have to know what we are feeling. This encouraged me to be more in touch with what I was feeling at any moment so I could clearly express what was going on.

We also need to consider that feelings are real but they are not reality.

This can be illustrated by the example of ten people witnessing the same event and all of them having different feelings /perspectives and narratives about it. Take looking at a painting or listening to a particular piece of music as an example. The feelings the artist wanted to engender in the recipient are one thing, what this brings up in the observer is another matter altogether. To put it another way we could say 'Beauty is in the eye of the beholder'.

If we meet someone in a social setting and after our meeting send them a text. Can we do this without any expectation? Whatever the response or lack of response are we able to remain in a stable state without any particular feelings being triggered in us. When there is no response this can create feelings of disappointment or feelings of fixation. If they respond very quickly we could be put off or get excited, there is no correct feeling response, feeling responses are not logical. They are being triggered by a combination of our past, present and our projection in to the future. When we only pay attention to what is actually happening moment by moment we start to experience something closer to reality. Rather than filling in the blanks with assumption, supposition and projection. So we slowly come to the conclusion that: feelings are real but they are <u>not</u> reality. Feelings arise either when we want something or there is something we don't want. We are obviously dividing things up in to good and bad and wanting the things we have called good and pushing away the things called bad.

GOOD AND BAD

"Allow rather than resist what arises in the present moment-inside or out. Let it be interesting rather than good or bad."

Dan Millman- The way of the peaceful warrior.

We cannot know what is good and bad we can only hold a limited opinion which may change as time passes. In The water course way Alan Watts recounts a story of a Taoist farmer whose horse runs away and it becomes clear that the interpretation of events can change at every turn:

"That evening the neighbours gathered to commiserate with him since this was such bad luck. He said, 'May be.' The next day the horse returned, but brought with it six wild horses, and the neighbours came exclaiming at his good fortune. He said, 'May be.' And then, the following day, his son tried to saddle and ride one of the wild horses, was thrown, and broke his leg. Again the neighbours came to offer their sympathy for the misfortune. He said, 'May be.' The day after that, conscription officers came to the village to seize young men for the army, but because of the broken leg the farmer's son was rejected. When the neighbours came in to say how fortunately everything had turned out, he said, 'May be.'"

Alan Watts, The watercourse way

We just don't know what is good and bad so if we skilfully relate to the situation with curiosity we can remain free of judgement. When we are working with this in our own lives looking curiously at what arises we can help those around us to relate to their situations more clearly by not getting drawn in to their judgements. When our default position is to seek to learn from the difficult experiences, and celebrate our positive experiences and the positive experiences of others. We go towards the difficult experiences, for example we look with curiosity at the person we are finding annoying to discover what they are reflecting back to us about ourselves. We are truly grateful for all the everyday miracles. Then we can relate to what is happening, rather than reacting in a dramatic way to continuous judgements. We start to remove the drama from our lives and live in a much more even way.

"As soon as you concern yourself with the 'good' and 'bad' of your fellows, you create an opening in your heart for maliciousness to enter. Testing, competing with, and criticizing others weaken and defeat you."

Morihei Ueshiba

Even if we drop this way of comparison and judgement for a few hours or even a day we can get the feeling of how this could be. To live outside of this dramatic story we are putting on to events. When we bring a genuinely curious attitude to everything we undo our fixation our habit of labelling everything. We then start to inquire in to life.

This can be particularly important when we come together with a partner. The man is usually driven by his sexual desire and tends to act in a straight line, moving towards his goal of sexual connection. If something comes up that the woman needs to deal with, a change of feeling or an issue, perhaps a past trauma. This usually arises as a feeling, which may take a while for words to form around the experience in order to express what is arising. If the man can meander curiously with the woman to discover what it is that has come up there is a genuine opportunity for deep intimacy to be explored between the couple.

Most often this kind of 'interruption' is experienced as 'bad' by the man, as the mood might be lost and sexual intimacy may not happen. The man's trajectory has been diverted; he might try all sorts of tricks including shame and anger at his partner to try to continue with his trajectory. When the soft inquiring nature of curiosity has the much greater capacity to explore and possibly unravel what has come up. This exploration then leads to a greater understanding of each other, which leads to greater intimacy.

If we take the word curious and break it down we get

" CUR(e) I o US".…. Cure I US and when we engage our curiosity rather than our judgement we can quell the drama in ourselves and others.

Curiosity brings us in to the present moment and has no end point, so keeps us continuously in to the moment. Through questioning skilfully we can learn from every situation, and when we learn from a mistake it is not a mistake it is a lesson. It is only if we do not learn that it is a mistake.

When we bring a state of tender curiosity and interest in all facets of the other we bring the opposite of an interrogation. We bring an invitation to opening. When we listen to the other there are often aspects that are charged with emotion that they will skip over and when we are listening with tender curiosity we feel these emotional crevasses that are being jumped across as they are spoken. This is what I mean by tender curiosity, when we ask "tell me about that experience" because we are really listening to the other. When we are maintaining an Alpha state the internal dialogue is disabled as the prefrontal cortex where the self-critical thought originates is less active. So we are able to listen with little or no inner dialogue of our own. This gives a much fuller presence to the other which is really our most precious gift to each other.

This curiosity breeds a much deeper intimacy and has the capacity to help each other unravel emotional and mental knots, when exercised skilfully. By being curious and making an exploration in to the other we develop greater understanding and understanding leads to greater care. Knowing the other builds kinship and expands our view of the possible ways to see the world and ways it can be responded to.

When we examine what we want and need from a relationship there are things that are obvious and then there are subtler qualities that we can miss.

It is similar in the early stages of a relationships that small interactions can set up or trigger patterns that can affect the ongoing relationship. We can cut off whole areas of communication with the other by an off-hand comment or lack of attention to some important issue they are raising. That makes them feel unsafe to be able to have that conversation.

Perhaps as a man we engage in something exciting and adrenalizing and want to share that with our prospective partner and it just creates trauma for the woman, like taking them for a ride on a motorbike or in fast car. This type of situation can lead to fear and mistrust. On the other hand it may 'sweep her of her feet'.

It is important that these issues can be discussed safely. Safe communication rests on our capacity for emotional sovereignty, owning our feelings and not taking the others emotions personally.

This quality of safety is a requirement for both parties. Both the feminine and the masculine needs to feel safe to open up and share. This invariably creates more intimacy. For the masculine who can often be less adept at communicating emotions, the whole business of sharing their inner aspect can hold a great deal of fear. This can come from having shared in the past and their innermost delicate concerns being fashioned into an emotional spear and thrown back into their heart. The imprint of this may have come from unconscious behaviour in the past from either or both parties. When a man is unable to listen to a woman, tries to fix, is defensive, or negates the woman's feelings instead of her feelings being grounded and received they can escalate. It is often at this point that the intimacy of the masculine becomes the ammunition to try to get him to hear her.

MEN AND FEAR OF INTIMACY

The masculine trajectory in relation to fear is that first he needs to deal with physical violence from other boys and men, this starts as boys. Then once a response to this is achieved in one of many ways, becoming strong, skilful, a joker, avoidance, making powerful friends, being superior, becoming a bully etc… This leads to dealing with the next layer of fear which is existential fear, fear of the supernatural; it is no accident that in most horror films the main protagonists are teenagers. As this is when both young men and women are starting to question what is beyond the physical. This can lead to much experimentation with alcohol and drugs or methods of changing state like meditation and visualisation. In this very easily influenced state they can join cults or religions in order to deal with this fear. They could also decide that there is nothing beyond the physical and follow the cult of scientism as then they are shielded by the belief that if it can't be measured it can't exist.

One of the things this book is trying to illustrate in the chapter on parenting is how we naturally move through the four main brainwave states as children. Our further exploration of these four states is down to us as they contain the main qualities and capacities that are presented in both the main religions and spiritual traditions around the world. The only exception to this is the Gamma state, associated with bliss and discovered amongst monks and nuns practicing Buddhist loving kindness meditations.

Only once this journey of discovery has been undertaken in

some form do men confront the fear of exposing their emotional selves, as they fear that the feminine who is much more skilful in this realm can destroy their delicate soft interior. Some of the ways this can happen are through, manipulation, shaming, sharing their intimate details with others, tying them in emotional knots etc...

Here is a recent poem about this masculine trajectory:

Courage to love

Would we rather stand on the battlefield?

Would we rather face the darkest night of the soul?

Than stand unguarded in front of the beloved,

The untramatised sisters wear their boundaries on the outside

The brother's boundaries are tied around their heart,

Their innermost secret, sometimes even to themselves,

The sisters healing is through beauty,

The recognition that the witnessing of the beauty of the earth,

Is a reflection of their inner beauty,

The brothers heal by facing the edge,

Returning with triumphant tales of power,

Of overcoming the self, of taking charge,

Yet are we tempered enough by griefs tender reminder,

That when we have stood over our shattered heart,

Broken, knowing there is no fixing it this time,

And hear it whisper, "Surrender to this feeling,

It was the one I wanted you to feel all along,"

That would unlock your hidden treasure,

Your soft golden heart, that shines with the power of the sun,

Then we have the courage to love,

To stand unguarded in front of the beloved

To listen, to feel, to receive, to journey in to the mystery,

To the last remaining edge where we may truly show up.

Safety for the woman requires a level of emotional stability
from the man. If he has developed the capacity to listen,

remembering that it is not about him in that moment, that just holding the space is his best response. She will feel received, another important consideration for her. She will in turn then be able to receive the man. As we mirror each other.

When two clear mirrors are placed opposite each other the reflection goes to infinity.

All this leaves is for the woman to feel loved. In the early stages of the relationship the man is so attentive that they both go to an event or out to dinner and the man's focus is entirely on the woman, half the film goes unwatched as he is gazing at her more of the time, food gets cold and goes uneaten etc.. For the masculine that is in this phase of full focused attention it is not often realised that it is the quality of their attention that really awakens the woman's reciprocal interest and she feels really loved and desired.

The next phase of the expression of love from the masculine is to get busy being a provider. This is through doing things for the woman, helping, fixing, driving, building, even providing a home and other resources. This shift can cause a problem as the man's focus can go so wholeheartedly in to these things that he forgets to give his woman the level of focus he gave her in the beginning of their relationship. The man feels he is expressing his love through all these other ways. The woman wonders where her man has gone and why he is so focused on doing rather than being. At this point it is worth re-establishing time to just be together with each other with nothing specific to do.

A great cause of friction in relationship is between the goal orientated more masculine way of doing and the feminine way of being in the flow. When the man enters the home space he is often still in efficiency mode and needs to be softened both in to flow and connection. His appearance in the home can be jarring and a cause of shock to the woman's system if she is in her flow.

Her first need is for connection, once this is established the man can even continue to be busy in the home space as long as his voice and actions are within the flow. The feminine flow and the Alpha or flow state are one and the same. Yet within the domestic environment it is much less noticed. By focusing on this I hope to bring this into both men's and women's awareness. When men and women both understanding their different relationship to flow they can understand and not take personally the behavioural traits of the other and can adapt their behaviour to the other's needs or requests from a place of understanding.

FEMININE FLOW

Women are so in the natural flow a lot of the time they are not even aware of this until it is broken by a loud noise or abrupt and jarring movements.

A friend of mine shared with me that he had 'just stood up' and his partner had got very upset with him. He is a big man and knows how to move powerfully. So on reflection I can see how this could be felt as a breaking of the flow for his partner. Yet as a man he was completely unaware that he could have done anything wrong.

When this friend shared this anecdote with me I did not understand about feminine flow. It was only six months later when I was invited to be part of a women only ceremony as the representative of the sacred masculine that I witnessed this. I have been in many men's ceremonies and this was different. A great deal of care was taken to make the whole experience beautiful smooth flowing and held with the heart. The opportunity to just listen to the beautiful elder who held the ceremony pray would have been enough for me. Yet I witnessed something throughout the ceremony that I just could not put any words around for several months. It was only when the contrast of the story my friend had told me of 'just standing up' that I realised what I had witnessed.

The quality of flow that women are naturally in was amplified by the number of women and the ceremonial context.

I later tried to explain this to a group of women and when I did they looked at me blankly. I then moved in a fast and powerful way (like my friend standing up) and raised my voice at the same time. In response to this all the women flinched. I then explained that I had broken the flow and they had all felt it, almost as a physical pain. Then they understood what I had been trying to mansplain.

The way this can play out in a domestic situation is that the woman asks the man to do the washing up. He obliges and goes about his washing up with much clanking of plates and cutlery. Once finished the man comes out of the kitchen and the woman asks him if he is alright. The man is confused, he has just done something that he thinks will please the woman and is met with a question about his emotional state. The woman's response comes from feeling that there is some unexpressed emotional issue that is not being talked about because the dishes were washed in a noisy way that was breaking the flow.

Even though this is a trivial example when we understand these different perspectives about each other we can avoid a great deal of friction.

When the man understands how he can disturb this resonance and how it affects the woman he has the opportunity to drop in to this flow around women. When a woman understands this she can reinterpret the man's behaviour as him not understanding or forgetting about this flow. This can then create more emotional space and a deeper sense of flow. It is no coincidence that the Alpha state is called the flow state.

What is also clear is that when moving silently in nature to get close to animals the hunter has to access this same quality of flow. Loud noises and jerky movements break the flow and will scare away the animals. One of the components of the Alpha breath dynamics comes directly from the practice of stalking animals in nature. The slowing down of the breath and movement are implicit once we start to move at one minute per step which is the speed we need to move to successfully stalk animals.

RECEIVING

We can all have an aversion to receiving, when someone compliments us we often rebuff the comment so as not to be seen as vain or arrogant. Yet we are not receiving the gift of the other person's positive energy. Imagine giving someone a present and them receiving it badly. This makes the giver feel bad breaking the flow of their energy to you. So when we do not receive well in relationship it can make our partner feel bad. Men find it very difficult to receive and similarly to ask for help. As this can make them feel less capable and self-sufficient.

This takes practice so run some experiments in receiving and asking for help: The next time you get a text message sending you hugs, receive them before sending any back. One way a Heartner of mine helped to encourage me in skilful receiving. Try receiving a compliment well rather than shrugging it off.

I have witnessed this difficulty in receiving even with homeless people who have barriers of pride and shame around receiving. Similarly I have witnessed people working with the homeless who have gained far more through giving than seems to equate with their actions. As if there were issues of guilt at play in motivating their actions of giving.

EMOTIONS ARE A SKILL

Let's look at this in a bit more detail as it was mentioned in the chapter 'Live'.

'Grief is a skill' Steven Jenkinson tells us, part of his reasoning is that we cannot pass through this life without loss. Without our loved ones dying, without falling in and out of love without growing and moving on from one state of being to another.

To help to understand the process of grief Elisabeth Kubler-Ross developed a model of seven stages that we move through. Though she describes them in sequence they can come in any order: Shock, Denial, Anger, Bargaining, Depression, Testing and Acceptance.

This already puts quite a few emotions on the list that we can develop our skill in relating to. What if all emotion was a skill if we developed a relationship with each one that allowed us to relate to the so called negative emotions skilfully? What would this look like?

If we were to engage with this approach, and did a roll call of all the so called negative emotions which would we choose to form a relationship with and what would the most useful relationship be?

Take a moment to consider this.

We are generally involved in pushing away what we don't like and trying to bring towards us the things we like. The Buddhists call it aversion and grasping. So if we were to flip this script and choose the emotion that was hardest to deal with, the one that underpins so many actions and choices. I would suggest the meanest negative emotion in the yard to deal with is fear.

In order to become skilful with our emotions we need to develop a relationship with them. The relationship we can enter into is one of learning, this leads to becoming skilful with the emotion. When we ask "What have you come to teach me this time?" we are engaging with and moving towards what we consider to be negative, instead of pushing it away. As we change our orientation to what we call negative emotions this starts to rewire our habitual emotional reaction and starts to turn it in to a response.

We are stepping on to the path of the warrior the minute we choose to take fear as our greatest teacher.

As we learn more from fear it matters less and less if it turns up as we will learn something from it. Then the fear will have a diminished effect on us the next time, as we learn what to do in the face of it again and again.

This helps us understand that all the so called negative emotions are teachers shrouded in various disguises. When we choose the meanest so called negative emotion in the yard to learn from we understand how to vanquish all the others.

Reaction/ response/choice

There seems to be a sequence of ways in which we relate to emotions:

Starting with what seems like a complete lack of choice and almost an addiction to the traumatised cycles we can be stuck in. These patterns or cycles are familiar even though they are usually extremely uncomfortable. Our fight, flight, collapse response may have been triggered. Here, we are in an acutely activated state. We can struggle to come out of these reactions without skilful assistance especially if our nervous system is in a state of constant triggering. We have become familiar with the chemical releases in our system and strangely need it to feel normal. If we are traumatised we can be hyper vigilant for the cause of our trauma and so inevitably find what we are looking for.

Then we have a situation that is considered more normal that of being caught in habitual unconscious reactions. We have more choice but it is not usually exercised very readily. Or it can come in to play after the fact when we see we have over reacted. The main strategy we can apply here is not to try to change anything. Instead to just observe ourselves carefully, to really pay attention to what we do and as we see ourselves more clearly we will find we change through observing ourselves. We then start to catch ourselves in the act and eventually can halt our unconscious reactiveness. On the way we need to be kind to ourselves as introducing this small amount of space into our awareness can encourage self-criticism. So know that each behaviour you bring into awareness even though you might not like it in yourself now has the potential to be let go of. When these behaviours are repeated again and again you will catch yourself a little bit earlier each time. So celebrate these little steps rather than sinking in to self-criticism.

Through creating more space within us by softening through meditation and or using the Alpha Breath Dynamics we can move towards a response rather than a reaction. When this is put together with the development of our emotional sovereignty i.e. owning what we are feeling, we become more adept at expressing our emotions. Then we start to respond rather than react.

"Between stimulus and response there is a space. In that space is our power to choose our response. In our response lies our growth and our freedom."

Viktor E. Frankl

The final stage is that we decide to choose our state, we become positive. This does not necessarily mean we are always happy just that we are prepared to face whatever arises with a positive attitude.

Emotional state	Relationship to emotion	Internal state	Relationship to space
Acute activation	Addiction	Trauma	Lack of choice
Unconscious Habit	Reaction	Stress	Normalised
Conscious Choice	Response	Calm	Spacious
Skilful action	Action	Equanimity	Empty

THE ISSUE IS IN THE TISSUE

We can have very selective memories of past events that can influence our present experiences. Because we tend to remember our emotional reactions very clearly as if they are live and happening now. This characteristic of the memory of emotional reaction is a somatic experience, so is stored in the whole body not just as a mental image.

When we are very empathetic and sensitive we can feel and experience the trauma of others. This could be from a piece of news coverage, or a historic report. Initially sensitives can find it difficult to separate out their feelings from reported feelings and the feelings of others. This sensitivity is a gift. It is a gift that can have extreme side effects unless we develop resilience alongside it.

It is however much harder to develop sensitivity than it is to develop resilience.

The first step is to develop skilful boundaries and this can be a lifesaving experience for a sensitive person. There is no such thing as too sensitive, there is only not resilient enough.

Feeling in to another is something that the feminine is set up to do, a woman has to be able to feel what her baby needs until it starts to speak at the age of two. This also means that lying to a woman is a bad idea as she will feel something is wrong even if she does not know the details. Setting up a state of cognitive dissonance where she is feeling one thing and being told something else.

BOUNDARY EXERCISE

We have explored the notion that mind moves energy. So when we set intentions we are effectively setting up a holding pattern for our energy. One effective way we can do this is to draw a large circle on a piece of paper. Placing with in the circle everything we want in our life. We then put everything we do not want outside the circle. When I first did this many years ago I only had one thing I had to put outside the circle and that was 'people stealing my energy'. As an empathetic person I would listen to others troubles and they would go away feeling great and I would be left with their feelings. It was hard for me to distinguish whose feelings were whose.

This felt like my energy was being stolen. Once I went through this process the whole thing started to shift.

This plays in to the notion of the warrior, as the warrior has already made certain decisions through their strategic approach before engaging. Once their strategy has been set out they then surrender to the unfolding of events.

'A warrior on the other hand, is a hunter. He calculates everything. That's control. But once his calculations are over, he acts. He lets go. That's abandon. A warrior is not a leaf at the mercy of the wind. No one can push him: no one can make him do things against himself or against his better judgement. A warrior is tuned to survive, and he survives in the best of all possible fashions.' "

Carlos Castaneda Journey to Ixtlan p135 the mood of the warrior.

SPACE HOLDING

As mentioned before there is a quality of intimacy that arises from tender curiosity. This is one aspect of how we can hold space for each other. In the initial love story at the beginning of this chapter we meet someone and are attracted because of our childhood patterns and triggers we proceed to project on to the other creating expectations. We see them in a particular light through our projections and want them to always be the image we project. There is a feeling that if they change from how they were when we first met them it will destabilise us or make us feel insecure. Yet we are all changing and growing all the time. Often in relationship this is ignored and when change occurs it is not skilfully received by the other. Instead it is felt as a threat to the status quo and can be actively discouraged.

A partner might say 'But you hate that' as we try something new or we have a revelation and it is met with 'yes I already knew that'.

This blocks our capacity to grow, to spread our wings and to support that change in the other.

Another aspect of our projection is when we see the best version of the other and it makes us want to change them to become what we can see in them. This can go either way it can be insidious or powerfully supportive. It is ultimately up to the other person to fulfil their potential. If we can hold the space in the right way with tender curiosity perhaps some of their emotional knots can untangle and they can reach their potential. If we have expectations bound to this or a sense that they owe us something because of our effort then we can end up feeling resentful even if they reach their potential.

However it is worth remembering this Spanish saying: 'If you come as a saviour you are going to be crucified'.

BREAKING THE PATTERNS OF PROJECTIONS

How would it be if we tried something different? Instead of projecting and holding the other in a familiar shape, we asked the question:

'Who are you now?' when we meet.

Rather than implicitly holding the idea: You must remain as the person I first met and am familiar with or if you change I will leave.

When we ask 'who are you now?' we are allowing space for the other to be in a state of becoming. Perhaps in the intervening time they had an epiphany and are never going to be the same again or they had a difficult experience and are in a state of trauma.

This way of receiving the other creates a state of energetic freedom and acceptance that supports growth and change. It breaks down our powerful projections and expectations. Even if they just left the room for five minutes and returned, holding this concept allows us to meet freshly every time. We move beyond expectation and projection, two things that cause us suffering if we engage in them. In relationship they diminish the other and block growth.

TRANSITIONS

Transitions are important moments that can hold all kinds of hidden expectation and trauma. We can cause unintended suffering and can form bad habits when we are unaware of how we are when we arrive to reconnect with our partner or leave our partner. Perhaps when our partner leaves our abandonment issues are triggered and reassurance is needed. Similarly when we leave for a journey together our different styles of preparation and leaving may bring us in to conflict. For example one is ready within minutes and the other needs advanced warning and takes much longer.

Also when we arrive perhaps we want to be received in a particular way, and yet we might tell the other that it does not matter if they are there or not when we arrive. Yet expecting them to know we want to be received.

Another common situation that occurs is that the masculine returns and enters the home space in a masculine way. He is still in doing mode with all that goes along with that. Somewhat like a bulldozer and there is no change of pace as he enters. What the feminine wants is connection on arrival. Yet when the masculine is in the mode of getting things done the 'to do list' is usually more important than the connection. Perhaps some reminder at the door to slow down and connect first might be required or tasking the feminine to remind the masculine to make a connection before continuing with his task orientated mind set. Once connection is made the masculine can continue on their way, unless there are other priorities.

This can also happen when the masculine is working in the home engaging in a task that demands that get it done type of energy. The masculine can ignore the ongoing need for connection and flow. This is one of the reasons having builders in the home can cause so much friction even when we are doing it ourselves whilst still living in the space.

Awareness and communication around these transitions creates space to process issues that can come up and helps both parties to implement strategies that support each other.

A situation that can occur when we reconnect after an absence is that the first comment is one of criticism. It is something that is joked about (within the context of the

Jewish Grandmother or the Mother in law) yet it happens often, this criticism is a way of cutting the other down to size or wrong footing them. It is a very painful way of communicating and is often unconscious. If we want to make others feel insecure it is usually because we are already feeling that ourselves.

Here are a few examples:

A mother sends her son two shirts; he goes to pick her up from the airport wearing one of them. Her first response is 'What's the matter you don't like the other shirt?'

A partner goes off for a week, in that time the other partner looks after the kids and repaints the kitchen, on returning the first response of the returning partner is, 'You missed a bit'.

A son phones his mother and the mother's first comment is 'If only you had phoned me yesterday'.

Whether these comments are funny or painful the underlying effect is to try to diminish the other.

We can choose to not take this type of thing personally or see the humorous side of it. Yet it can set the tone of the interaction. I have given a few examples yet there are many that have been left out. In order to understand the issues that come up for you and the other you are with here is an exercise to try.

TRANSITION EXERCISE

This exercise is to move through the next transition you have to make with full awareness. Notice what arises in you and what arises in the other. Do this with curiosity rather than judgement. Give space to yourself to see what is yours. Observe lovingly what occurs in the other.

Also experiment with entering in different ways and see what happens.

For example practice the Alpha breath dynamics before entering.

Pause and ground yourself before entering.

Make sure your needs are met before entering, if you are hungry eat something etc..

As you enter put your entire focus on the other for at least ten minutes before doing anything else.

Before entering run through all the things you are grateful for in relation to the other.

If you are anxious about entering imagine the interaction being harmonious before entering.

Before entering soften in to your heart.

These are a few experiments to try I am sure you can come up with many other ones.

NOT FEELING LOVED ENOUGH

Finally I want to talk about the main wound we all carry which is that we do not feel loved enough. It is this wound that causes us to seek out the other and expect them to be in charge of our happiness by loving us enough. We are in charge of our own happiness it is only down to us.

Imagine how it would be if we felt loved enough and did not need validation as we were filled with love already. Then perhaps we would be seeking another who too was filled with love who wanted to just be with us, without the usual sense of grasping for love from the other. We talk about falling in love could we rise in love?

When we consider where our bodies come from what fuels them and makes them function well we can discover the ground of our being. From this ground springs our physical, mental and emotional selves. That ground of our being is the air we breathe the food we eat and the water we drink. This means that we are being loved in to existence in every moment by this ground of being. Without it we cannot exist. So if we can feel how we are being loved in to existence in every moment by this beautiful miraculous Earth then perhaps we might feel loved enough. It is a conspiracy of love that makes life possible. And that conspiracy does not stop at the Earth, as the phosphorous in our bones is made in the stars. So the whole universe is conspiring to love us in to existence.

Just feel that for a moment.

This is what is actually happening, yet we are too busy focused on the negative to even notice this.

Run an experiment for a week by spending some time each morning reminding yourself of this and let the feeling grow in you. Then see if you can meet the other filled with that sense of love no longer grasping for it from them.

This universe loves you

In the vastness of space

A heart beats to the rhythm of love

Birthed by a harmonious spirit song

The flesh that surrounds it

Is the love of the Earth

The bones that animate it

Is the love of the Stars

The blood that flows through it

Is a river of love

Its very existence is the proof of love

And all this is happening in you too

And you ask me if I love you

And I say the whole universe loves you

And you say, you are being evasive

Ok I say, *this* universe loves you.

4

PARENTING

From when we are born we move through a spectrum brainwave states that change as we grow and develop. There is various information available on this subject, yet I suspect that these developmental stages are somewhat different for each individual. The accounts I have found have some variation. So what I provide here is a general framework that helps us look at the transition of brain wave development. This allows us to relate more skilfully to our children and young adults. Knowing the predominant state they are in at their various ages. It also offers insight in to our own experiences of childhood and shows how natural access to the different brainwave states is. Research in to child development has shown a very interesting series of transitions that a child makes in their brain wave development from birth to puberty.

When a child is born and for the first two to four years they are predominantly in a Delta state. This is the slowest and deepest brainwave state from 0.5 HZ to around 4. In this state the growth hormone is triggered, and by the age of four children's brains are ninety five percent grown. The word I associate with the Delta state is Awe. Interestingly when we encounter a new born or young child, we can spontaneously come in to a state of awe. There is a quality of purity and unconditioned nature that they exude. As they have newly arrived and are mostly unconditioned. The pure unconditioned state of Delta is the closest resonance to what gets called awakening or enlightenment and we are gifted with four years of this state. Even strangers can come up to us when we have a new born to adsorb some of this radiance. This is one of the great gifts that the baby or young child brings and spending time with them helps us re-experience this pure state.

They are predominantly in this state for the first four years of their lives. They struggle to control their bodies and do not speak for the first two years. Yet we can have a wordless communication with them when we mirror the Delta state. As adults we rarely access this state. We might find that we wake from sleep occasionally feeling deeply refreshed with no recollection of any dreams and we may have dropped in to this state in sleep. Our capacity to access this state consciously as adults can be limited. If we have practiced a lot of meditation we may recognise this non conceptual feeling state.

At the age of four the child's imagination kicks in and they start to play imaginary games as they are transiting in to the Theta brain wave range 4-8 HZ. If we were to try to reduce this state to a single word the one I would choose would be wonder. During this phase we can communicate with our children through the imagined and imaginary. As it is a gateway in to this state for adults.

I was watching a mother struggling to put sun cream on her daughter one morning at a festival. I watched for ten minutes while she tried in vain to cover her in sun protection and the woman's son wriggled uncomfortably away from her attempts. After ten minutes I went over and said to her son 'I bet you can't stay as still as a statue for two minutes' he immediately froze and his mother stood shocked for a moment before seizing her chance to finish the job.

When children are in this phase we can turn everything in to a game. I remember one house hold where whenever any of the children said 'that is mine', the parents would encourage everyone to lie down on the floor because there was a 'Land Mine' this was how they had creatively chosen to tackle this all to frequent parental experience.

Einstein one of the preeminent scientists of our age said:

"If you want your children to be intelligent read them lots of fairy stories, if you want them to be really intelligent read them more fairy stories".

He is saying feed their imagination as he wrote that his major discoveries were from thought experiments what we would call visualisation now. He then put words around the experiences in order to be able to explain them to others. Then finally figured out the maths, not the other way round, he also said:

"Logic will get you from A to B imagination will take you everywhere else".

I was once at a campsite with a large group of friends. Many of our children were there and they ran off and became somewhat feral. I witnessed a situation that was becoming a bit like the lord of the flies, as a large group of boys began to gang up on one boy who was not as physical. He was more bookish and creative. Just as they came towards him he drew his imaginary sword, they also grabbed their imaginary weapons and an imaginary battle took place. This young boy had defended himself with his imagination. Once their fight came to an end the boy's asked him what they could play next and he became the one who came up with the games they all played.

As well as this imaginary skill there are very real characteristics that come with this brainwave state. We can have boundless energy and have the capacity to know things without knowing how we know them, a quality of extrasensory perception. The Theta state is akin to the state shamans have accessed for millennia.

As adults we access this in our dream state, we generally experience two hours of rapid eye movement (R.E.M.) sleep per night. In the dream state as in Theta there is no physical limitation and no time. In our dreams we can be in the past or future just as easily as the present, we can fly or breath under water etc.. This is a magical time for us as children where many of our life dreams and aspirations are planted. This is one of the reasons we feel our childhood is so magical. As adults we can support this by playing along, and using play as a way to encourage our children to act in ways that we would like them to behave.

Children at this stage are very sensitive and are usually learning from our behaviour more than what we communicate. Interestingly when we lie to our children especially at this age they can feel it and can sense if we are telling the truth. So their internal compass can either be orientated through our integrity or be bent out of shape by us not speaking the truth to them. Sometimes as a parent we might miscommunicate for our own convenience. Unfortunately this can create cognitive dissonance in our children. The reason for this is that we all have an inner compass and if our parents lie to us when we are children this can mean we misread our inner compass. It can however be recalibrated, I talk about this in the chapter 'Live' under body compass.

Having said this, there are many things with in the adult world that we would naturally keep from them that do not have a direct effect on their lives or inner compass.

The next shift happens around 7-8 years and continues till around 12-13 this brain wave state 8-12 HZ is the Alpha range. This is the state of calm and focused or the flow state. Children will want to engage in more complex games and tasks for their own sake, tasks that build skills and are adsorbing. I remember starting to be interested in Chess, board games and building Air-fix airplanes. As parents we can also encourage activities that we find helpful to access the flow state. Things like music, art and sport.

This is also the time to encourage more time in nature as nature is resonating at around this frequency. If they become comfortable in natural environments this becomes an excellent resource later on for their mental wellbeing and physical health. There is mounting research to demonstrate that psychological resilience is built through interaction with nature. A study run by Exeter University of twenty thousand people concluded that two hours in nature a week had a significantly positive effect on both physical and mental health (Mathew P White et al 2019). For millennia children have naturally spent most of their time out of doors and only in recent times has access to nature become such an issue. We can encourage an interest in birds or gardening or other wildlife. There are some excellent books on nature connection games for children and many games we can play indoors that can give us a way into understanding nature.

The next state change that occurs is at around twelve to thirteen, this is the change in to the Beta state which is resonating at around 13-26 HZ. This happens around puberty and is accompanied with the sudden development of self-consciousness; this can be very alarming for the child, especially with the current social media trends. If they have spent lots of time in nature they will have already created a connection with a supportive non-judgmental environment that helps them maintain an Alpha state.   Sharing Alpha breath dynamics with them as a tool to reduce anxiety can then help them access the flow state whenever they need to. This has huge capacity to ease their transition in to the beta state. It is the prefrontal cortex that is switched on by this brain wave shift which creates these self-critical habits. Similarly the commencement of what we call internal dialogue is brought on by this shift.   The beta state is considered the normal state for humans. I consider the Alpha state to be the natural state for humans. When we access the Alpha state the prefrontal cortex is silenced.

Once embedded in the beta state our education system which sees competition and academic achievement as the main goal, unconsciously focusses solely on this state, not realising that the Alpha state provides a much more relaxed state for the students and a greater capacity to retain information and be creative. As creative subjects and sport are relegated to less important we are training our children out of the use of the Alpha state. This is setting them up for a life of stress and anxiety.

As our children turn in to teenagers they want to explore aspects of the adult world to do with state change. So they experiment with alcohol and drugs that they see and feel are changing the state of the adults around them. If we can teach them how to access these states naturally and safely we answer their questions before their own experiments can get them in to challenging and difficult situations or worse in to addiction and crime.

If we go back to the transition from Theta to Alpha, to examine a situation that is becoming more and more common, we discover that this transition can sometimes not happen and have some quite extreme consequences. I have trained many youths and children and watch carefully how they behave. After watching many children with ADD and ADHD I began to conclude that they must still be in a Theta state, not yet having transited in to the Alpha state.

A few years after I began to consider this I discovered that young people with ADD and ADHD have been found to exhibit a dominance of Theta brain waves. Retraining them to be able to change their state into Alpha has shown good results. This has largely been done with brain wave entrainment. Now it is possible to use the natural approach of Alpha breath dynamics for this purpose.

The excessive energy of attention deficit hyperactivity disorder is also a characteristic of the Theta state. When we use this consciously we can access far more energy than normal and find we don't need to recharge. People with

ADHD also exhibit a lack of focus, but with this comes a great deal of sensitivity both to other people's moods, or as I discovered to the sudden appearance of a hawk overhead in dense woods, or to uncovering the hiding place of an instructor. It is a kind of hypervigilance. There are downsides to the Theta state, the daydreaming quality that it holds can lead to an unfocused lack of presence in the moment, and also the slower brainwave pattern is sometimes associated with depression. When we are stuck in the Theta brainwave state and are not experiencing the other parts of the spectrum it seems to become a problem.

I hypothesised that this is caused by trauma having been experienced during the period of development when the child is between the ages of 4 to 8 when they are predominantly in a Theta state. This trauma then somehow blocks the child's ability to develop the Alpha brainwave pattern.

The Theta brainwave state may feel safer with its imaginary context, access to a great deal of energy and with the capacity to feel less pain. It is in Theta that we can develop the skill of remote viewing so exiting the body when confronted with unpleasant circumstances is not uncommon, leading to dissociation. Theta also gives us deep access to our intuition making it possible for us to receive information that there is no way we could consciously know. This can provide information to the child that can keep them safe in situations that have the potential to be traumatic or dangerous for them. With this hypothesis comes the added issue that when someone who has remained in a Theta state due to traumatic circumstances manages to access an Alpha state their trauma may resurface.

I was at an outdoor event and two young men approached the space I was teaching in and asked if they could roll a cigarette out of the wind. I got talking to the two young men; it was clear from the behaviour of one of the young men that he had A.D.H.D. The other was a gypsy boxer. I offered to show the young man my simple intervention that I had only recently developed. He was very reluctant and then after a few minutes he agreed. It turned out he had Asperger's and could feel my intention was good. After a few minutes of practice he was dramatically changed. He sat holding his rolled cigarette like a Buddha. He said he had never felt so calm in his whole life.

It was a minute or so after this that he broke down in tears, telling me and his friend that he had been sexually abused as a child and had never told anyone before. His friend exclaimed, "Oh Mate" and put his arm around him, It was a precious moment of healing for the young man.

This experience both added weight to my hypothesis and showed that if we are working with someone who may be exhibiting A.D.H.D. symptoms that are caused by extensive trauma that professional support should be sought to support this transition.

We need to bear in mind that children between the ages of 4-8 are generally quite sensitive and many things could constitute a trauma to them that can block the natural transition to the Alpha state.

PREVIOUSLY HELD ASSUMPTIONS ABOUT FLOW

I cannot claim any scientific credentials though I have run multiple experiments and my results are reproducible through the Alpha breath dynamics even by those with A.D.H.D.

Csikszentmihalyi the author of "Flow" 1990, a widely respected work, suggests that this group of children with attention disorders either have a genetic predisposition, a chemical imbalance or have not been brought up with the family characteristics that encourage flow behaviour. What I have found does not support this view.

Flow Page 84

"Some individuals might be constitutionally incapable of experiencing flow….Part of the answer probably has to do with innate genetic causes."

Csikszentmihalyi puts forward a series of very useful characteristics that I examine in the chapter about work, these characteristics have been extrapolated from studying other people's capacity to access the flow state. My perspective is rather different as it has arisen from studying and teaching how to access these states myself. This has helped me gain insight from a different angle that offers an alternative perspective.

Csikszentmihalyi even goes as far as to say on page five of his book 'Flow' that it is not possible to offer quick ways to access the flow state through a book. I hope to have proved him wrong with my findings in the first chapter.

Caveat

I feel that I need to add in a little note here as I share several experiences of raising my own progeny in this next section. Firstly an apology to them for sharing things that are quite personal yet help to illustrate multiple points of great value. Secondly to say that I have made many mistakes in my relationships and in my parenting, the incidents I share here are high lights, things that have worked. When things go right it is a combination of insight and action that come together to produce a good result. I could fill several volumes of things that did not go so well.

A POSITIVE SUGGESTION

One thing that is known by N.L.P. and trance practitioners is the power of positive suggestion. If I ask you not to think of a purple elephant, in order to comprehend my statement you have to think of a purple elephant. The unconscious does not register the words 'not' and 'don't'. This means that when we say to a child 'don't do that', they only hear 'Do that'. By making a positive suggestion we get round this difficulty and we can also do some lasting good for our children. If when our child climbs up in to a tree or a lamp post we say 'don't do that you will fall off' we are implanting this suggestion. We could say 'be careful and make sure you have a good grip' 'climb as high as you feel safe' 'Keep your balance' etc.. My sons who I have spoken to like this, their whole lives just came third and fourth respectively in their local bouldering centre's climbing competition. The implications for how we talk to our children are immense.

It is like a spell we are casting on their subconscious. The things a parent says can implant themselves very deeply in the child and can lurk there for a life time. These comments or spells can have very specific and sometimes long lasting effects. Some of the work I do is uncovering these fulcrum points which often have a statement embedded in them. I then work to help the person transform this negative statement in to a statement of power.

I luckily learned about positive suggestion just before my first child was born choosing my words as carefully as possible with in the circumstance. When my now young adults were children and they would hurt themselves I would say 'you heal up really fast' to encourage this behaviour.

The mentor that I learned this from is a very skilful trance practitioner he came with his family one year to a family camp I was running. At one point a young boy was brought to me with a cut that had turned to septicaemia, the child had been given many courses of antibiotics previously to attending the camp which had affected his immune system. My mentor came over while I was examining the child and explained that he was a trained paramedic, this statement established him as an authority he then made a very simple suggestion. He looked the child in the eyes and said 'you have really good blood' no one else even noticed this suggestion. I had to send the child to the local hospital to be checked out, but he went with a powerful suggestion that his blood was good.

This mentor after assisting in a S.A.S. training exercise was diagnosed with frost bite in his hand and foot, the doctors said that they could only save him if they amputated his hand and foot. He said no and proceeded to heal his hand and foot using herbs, his own form of trance therapy and meditation. I saw him a month or so after the exercise and his finger nails and toe nails had turned black and fallen off. They grew back eventually and he still has his hand and foot to this day. He returned to see the doctor who had diagnosed him and showed him his hand and foot were perfectly fine.

The doctor's response was, 'you can't have had frost bite in the first instance' My mentor replied 'then why were you going to amputate?' There is a great deal of power in how we talk to ourselves and how we talk to others.

How we use language when we communicate with ourselves is something we can pay close attention to. The tone and words we use can have a strong impact. When we criticise ourselves and believe the feelings and story we tell ourselves we are writing our script for the future.

'I am a failure', 'I never have enough money', and 'I am really bad at relationships'. These are some of the conversations we have with ourselves, even speaking many of them out loud when we are talking to others. It is not easy to change these habits, to rewrite the negative statements and spells we are casting on ourselves.

(If you go back to the start of the previous sentence you will notice that I stated 'it is not easy to…' This is using a positive reinforced statement. The subconscious does not register the 'not' so here the suggestion is that it is easy to change these behaviours.)

We can rewire our script much like making a positive spelling of the statement.

'I will learn from this failure' or 'I have not succeeded yet'.

'I might not feel as if I have enough money right now and yet all my needs are being met in this moment' or

'I don't have much money at the moment 'and yet I always land on my feet' or 'I don't have much money at the moment and who knows what is around the next corner'

'I feel that I am <u>no</u> good at relationships, perhaps there are things I can learn from my failures' or 'I am getting better at relationships'.

I might be a bit dyslexic but this kind of spelling I find I am really good at.

These are not necessarily affirmations they are ways of catching ourselves when we are being unkind to ourselves. We can try to treat the self as an honoured guest.

THE MYTH OF CONSISTENCY

As a parent we think that we have to be consistent in how we parent. Like King Solomon able to weigh up and judge situations as they arise with wisdom and sobriety; always offering the same responses to our children so they feel safe and can rely on us like the banks of a river always steering them in the right direction. We may be able to maintain this most of the time however the idea of consistency is ultimately untenable as we have good days and bad days. There are times when we have lots of energy for play and other times when we are exhausted and short tempered.

We can only realistically be consistent with how we are feeling in the moment. This means that we can be consistently real with our children. Rather than holding a fake consistency that is an ideal we can crucify ourselves upon. By skilfully communicating our energy levels or emotional state with our children we create a resilient consistency that allows room for us as a parent.

Children are sensitive to their parent's emotional state. So by communicating clearly with them they get less confused by our actions. One of the draw backs or possible gains with this is that we need to know what we are feeling in the moment. If we are not used to keeping track of our feelings this can be difficult to start with. We might have had to bury our feelings in order to just get on with the demands of life. So this is a good time to slow down and actually acknowledge to ourselves when a feeling surfaces. This will help with all our relationships.

THE BEHAVIOUR IS THE MESSAGE

A number of years ago my oldest son asked me if I would buy him a game on his X-box. I agreed and gave him my credit card details. I was not using my credit card much at the time, so checked my credit card bills about seven months later. Only to discover that twelve hundred pounds had been spent by him on my credit card. When I discovered the amount I was furious and am glad he was not present to witness my response.

Once I had calmed down, I began to question what it was he was asking of me by this act. I realized, he was firstly saying that he did not understand the value of money. Secondly, I felt he was asking to be mentored into how to come into the world of work and earning a living. So when I confronted him with the discovery of his spending spree, I explained that I realised he had done it on purpose, that it was not a simple mistake. That he could either pay me back, by working and paying me, or he could work with me and work off the debt.

Because of this we spent a lot of time together over the following period. I was running several festivals a year at the time, so I asked him to help with this and of all the festival helpers I had he was the most reliable and consistently helpful. I felt he was worth paying a certain wage per day which for his age was a good amount. He then realised what his value was and began after a while to get other work and to charge his employers the same amount. After a while I changed our arrangement so that I would pay him half the wages he would have earned working for me and the rest would go to pay off the debt so he would come out at the end of the event with some money in his pocket.

At one event that my son was helping at, we had some helpers on site, including a single mum and her rather disruptive son. I had to leave site to get various supplies and on my return found my son on the job I had left him doing, not only was he doing the job but also mentoring the younger disruptive boy into helping him. It was after this that the disruptive lad no longer caused any trouble. I realized at this point that my strategy was working, seeing my son mentoring this disruptive lad. He was passing on what had been passed to him, by including this young boy in the process of setting up the festival he felt part of it and so had no need to cause a problem after that.

Three years later he had paid off the full amount and we have developed a great working relationship. At the last festival I ran in Devon one of the greatest pleasures of the whole event, was putting up and taking down the main marquee with just my two sons.

Had I just got angry with him, I would have damaged our relationship at a time when it was quite fragile and nothing would have been accomplished. By trying to understand what he was telling me, through his actions, we were able to move through a complex and difficult situation positively, creating many opportunities for us to spend lots of time together. He also began to understand how to enter the field of work and to get a measure of his self-worth.

PARENTAL HOLDING AND RITES OF PASSAGE

Perhaps you have had an experience where you return to your parental home, and while you are there you revert to all kinds of childish behaviours. Behaviours that you thought you had overcome as they only seem to occur when you are in the presence of your parents. This is one of the reasons that a family Christmas or other celebration can be so emotionally explosive.

There is a saying: "If you think you are enlightened go home"

I mention in the chapter on love how to break the patterns of projection and expectation we have with each other by asking the question 'Who are you now?'

One place where we all have experience of this kind of holding is in our relationship with our parents. They have expectations, dreams and projections around us and our future. The disappointment we can feel, or lack of acceptance and criticism when we do not meet their expectations. Even when their holding of us as 'children' well in to our later years can inhibit our individuation and development. Sometimes it is only when they pass that we feel this energetic holding lift. Like an energetic inheritance.

Rites of passage were used to mark the transition points from child to adult. To encourage the child to enter the world of the adult and to allow the parent to feel that shift in their young person and even grieve for the loss of their child as they became a man or a woman.

For girls and women there is a natural rite of passage that takes place, the beginning of menstruation. So there is a clear point that can be marked and celebrated where guidance from the mother and other trusted women can hold a space for this transition. If this is well tended it will reduce the likelihood of this event producing shame, anxiety and confusion.

I remember clearly two points in my daughter's transition to young adulthood. The first happened when we went for the first time to the opera at Glyndebourne. We lived in Lewes near Glyndebourne, and a good friend offered me two tickets to a not particularly well known opera. I was in my early forties at the time and wanted to see what all the fuss around opera was about. I took my teenage daughter with me. I was deeply touched by the experience, the richness of the sound of the orchestra and the emotive power of singing. The stage set was amazing too we could see through the stage like it was made of ice and solidified underneath were giant red flowers embedded under the surface. In the interval my daughter companied of really bad stomach cramps. Thankfully my

Dad radar was working as out of the blue I suggested that her periods might be starting.

The next day my daughter's mother rang up saying she had had a dream about our daughter and that she was covered in red rose petals (a bit like the scene from the film: American beauty). I told her about the previous day's events and the symbols of her dream became clear. Her mother had felt the transition so I returned my daughter to her mother so she could honour the transition in to becoming a woman.

The second experience was on a rite of passage camp I was holding. We had a mixed group of boys and girls including my daughter. I had been running these camps for several years by this time. Some family friends had brought their children to undergo the process and they had also brought an older youth who was the son of a friend of theirs.

A very interesting dynamic started to develop between the children who had come to undertake the rite and this young man who felt he was past the point of engaging with the process. A tug of war ensued between my attempts to engage the children in the process and this youth pulling them away from it as if it had no value.

It took me quite some attention to understand that this youth felt like he had no place with in the process. He was certainly not a child and was already on his way to being a young adult. Because of this he kept disrupting the process and drawing the others away from being engaged.

Eventually I found a role for him, as a fire keeper for the sweat lodge that was the start of the rite of passage. The role honoured him as a young adult and made him a supporter of the rite. At this point all the others became fully invested in the process.

As my daughter emerged from the lodge about to go on her quest she called to me and asked if I would get her a pair of socks. She stood on the thresh hold of becoming a young adult and I was suddenly overcome with such a wave of grief that I was losing my little girl. I replied that I could get her socks this one last time and after the rite she would have to get her own socks.

As parents we can hold our children back by continuing to refer to them as our children or babies etc.. I now refer to my 'children' as young adults as a way of encouraging them in to their own self sovereign state. It is out of respect that I refer to and address my young adults in this way. This is an invitation for them to step in to this roll rather than when they are around me to feel drawn back in to their childish persona. There is still a great deal of playfulness and affection in our interactions and plenty of room for responsibility to grow.

"They are the sons and daughters of Life's longing for itself. They come through you but not from you, and though they are with you yet they belong not to you."

Kahlil Gibran

STILL A CHILD AT FIFTEY

I was attending the wedding of a friend and during the proceedings my Mother innocently exclaimed 'How lovely to have all my children here'. I proceeded to say that as I was fifty it did not feel very respectful to me to be referred to as a child. My mother said nothing in response, until seven months later. The next Christmas I drove the five hours to visit her on Christmas day. I arrived with a present, and after the usual greetings we sat down with a cup of tea and a minced pie. It was then the issue of me claiming not to be her child came up and with full emotional charge she said 'how could I possibly say I was not her child, as she had given birth to me'. I listened fully, without defence, criticism, or trying to raise any counter point. When she stopped I asked 'Is there anything else you need to tell me?'

It was several months later that she confided in me that in her life of seventy four years no one had ever said 'Is there anything else you need to tell me?' after she had expressed herself with charge. I felt that I had not acted in any way like a child in the face of this type of expression I listened without defending myself and made space for any other issues that might be lurking to be aired. This served to unequivocally make the point that I fully inhabit my adult self.

Extract from True Nature about Rites of passage

The young boys are called by the elders to meet by the central tree, in the middle of the village. The mothers wail and cry, some cannot let go of their sons…the elders have to hold the mothers back restrain them. The mother's grief fills the air a tearing to the bone, a terrifying fierceness, at the loss of their boys, their children, their babies.

The elders make a break for it with the bewildered youths following. The youths are unsure of the next step, confused at their role in the tribe. Their growth in to self-consciousness no longer allows them to feel safe in the gender fluidity of childhood, of moving between the women's and men's camps. Wanting guidance from the elders, to be shown how to be strong in the world, respected by their peers and yet able to express the same patience and love their fathers showed them. The youths yearn to feel worthy, to find their gift their power, to live up to the promise of life and the stories they have been told round the fire late in to the night under the vastness of stars. They know how the earth supports their lives as everything is gathered or fashioned from the land on which they live and how to celebrate their life. They have heard stories of how spirit speaks to the worthy guiding them with beautiful and subtle clues, helping them to understand the intricate relationships between humans and their many non-human brothers and sisters; leading the hunters to the deer, steering the tribe away from danger or the simple daily communications of gratitude with the ancestors, earth, water, fire and air.

The elders lead the youths deep in to what they now experience as wilderness to return them home to the bosom of mother Earth, so that where ever they set foot on their return will be their home. The youths, are now eager, curious, excited and terrified in equal measure. The youths are seeking the next step for themselves they have no grief of the loss of their childhood only the promise of a life lived with connection to the vastness. An understanding not just of the workings of nature and survival but also, of their inner landscape of its depth and mystery.

They are brought to the elder's fire, held in a circle and taught the mysteries of life, nature, spirit and the heart. They would be taught through stories, laughter, communion, ceremony, powerful searching questions and life threatening challenges. In the times before time it would have taken many moons to be made ready to complete the final challenge, to Quest, to start to ask their question of life.

The youths would have sat alone far from their known lands, exposed to the elements, fasting, seeking guidance from the great mystery, the source. They had to push past tiredness, past hunger and thirst, through boredom, past the stations of irritation, annoyance and anger, in to vulnerability. Suffering strange incomprehensible dreams, speaking in tongues, speaking in silence, and then at last crying deep from within the broken heart of the forsaken, calling for true guidance for a life to be lived with purpose. And only then finally finding total surrender and letting go. No expectation, just gratitude for the release for the opportunity to pray for space. And from that allowing of the not knowing something stirs a subtle voice, a feeling a murmur, from the strangely silent land. The whisper of the ancestors calls to attention, to pay attention. The sudden appearance of the stag through the mist, the eagle's eerie cry or the dewdrop on the spider's web illuminated by the rising sun they unexpectedly stumble upon their grander self. Beyond whom they thought themselves to be. Like a giant gong being struck deep within.

Now remembered, born back to Earth mother and Spirit father, no longer just the child of their birth parents but a child of mystery, a child of the universe. Through their humility, letting go, they have shown worthiness to see a vision of becoming, recognition of their gift their passion, revealed as a path to becoming Human.

The youths return weak in body, but with their spirit shining. Tenderly they carry the treasure of their search, their quest, though not yet able to see their gift, and so they tell the story of their journey to the elder's. Wide eyed and with tears running down their wrinkled cheeks the elders hear the tales. Nodding and reflecting back the beauty, the courage the gift and the young men begin to see themselves reflected in the elder's eyes, in the elder's hearts.

The young men are brought back to the village, and the whole village comes to welcome, to receive to celebrate the heart full, young men. The mothers weep for their sons safe return, they can no longer call them children, or their babies, the mothers and fathers have felt the grief the loss and have accepted that now they are expected to support the new status of the fledgling adults.

Through the act of questing it is possible to develop the process of gaining wisdom from life's experiences. When this is carried through life it brings one to the door of elder hood. There is a difference between growing old and growing wise and it is inherent in this type of natural contemplation, as it teaches us how to make meaning from life's experiences.

WRONGS OF PASSAGE

THE OTHER SIDE OF THE COIN

"Something in the adolescent male wants risk, courts danger, goes out to the edge – even to the edge of death."
— Robert Bly, Iron John: A Book About Men

I was returning from a night out, with a few pints of larger in me. It was cold and I pulled my leather jacket tightly around my neck as I walked home. My hair was cropped short as I had been training for my brown belt. A young man approached me "You look like a hard bastard, can you help me??!!" he said…As a martial artist, I felt like I was as member of 'the moral up-liftment society' so I asked what the problem was. The young man explained that he and his friend had got into a taxi to go home and realised they did not have enough money to pay for the taxi. So they asked to be brought to a cash point to get some cash out and instead were driven round the back of the buildings we were in front of and thrown out of the taxi and beaten up by a gang of youths.

I agreed to help him look for his friend as the young man I was talking too had run away from the gang of youths and was worried that his friend could be in a critical condition. We walked around the block looking for his friend and found no sign of him. We got back to where we had first met, on the corner of Jamaica Street, and there across the road was the taxi. It was parked in front of a newsagent with all the shutters down except for the front door. In the door way were the youths who had attacked this young man.

He marched straight across the street and confronted the

youth in charge who at my estimate was the oldest at around eighteen. Bold I thought, but stupid, and somewhat unwillingly I crossed the street to back him up. As I came on to the pavement space between the taxi and the open door way the gang surrounded us. Using one of the few principles I had learned from my kung fu training I held up my hands in a non-threatening way saying "let's just all stay calm", The principle relies on the understanding that maintaining a proper distance from a would be attacker means that nine times out of ten it is possible to defend an attack, while if they are allowed within range nine times out of ten they can strike before they can be defended against.

The young man asked "What have you done with my mate?" "We put him in the f*****g B.R.I.(Bristol Royal Infirmary) and we are going to put you there to if you don't f*** off ". Moments after this a foot flicked out of the door way and caught this young man under the chin. He stumbled back passed where I stood, seeing an opportunity another of the youths stepped in and punched the young man. By this point the young man was passed the end of the taxi and into the road. Another youth pulled out a bike chain and wacked the young man around the ribs, at this point he ran off. He was alive, perhaps a fractured jaw, a cracked rib, but alive I thought.

I was left standing amongst these youths, I looked at them, they were thirteen to sixteen years old they were children, they were not young men. They were acting like a pack of dogs. Even the eighteen year old was acting out of pain. They had no other way of earning peer respect or finding their place in the tribe, their only road was violence.

I assessed the situation as I stood amongst five of these youths. A chain had been pulled out the next step in the escalation of the situation was that a knife could be next. I was confined by the taxi and a lamppost so no spinning techniques were possible, the best way I thought of dealing with several of them at once. Yet I had maintained my space the whole time and even though I stood amongst them none of them had found a way to attack.

They were youths, no they were children, I thought, how could I possibly attack a group of children.

I decided to walk away, to try to show that fighting was unnecessary. That one could be in the midst of this type of aggression and leave with a powerful dignity. I began to walk away with full attention if anyone had tried anything I would have had no mercy. And I think they felt the powerful meekness that I chose to express. The leader called "leave him alone" as I walked off.

I left with a profound feeling of sadness, no adrenalin response, just deep sadness, that these young men, these boys had no other way to express themselves. The sadness came from recognition that as there was no rite of passage for them they had created a wrong of passage. They had the sense of community, the camaraderie, the hierarchy, yet they were steering themselves down a path without heart. One of creating terror and fear rather than dealing with their own, their pain inflicted on others, the continuation of the trauma they were feeling. This type of misunderstanding of the transition from youth to adult is prevalent in the hazing that goes on in sports teams, university fraternities and many other situations. Ignoring this turning point turns this

powerful life rite in to a pale reflection at best and a
dangerous sanctioning of psychotic behaviour at worst. We
currently live in a society of uninitiated men and it creates a
very unsafe and dangerous society. It becomes a society of
adolescents rather than one where men are tempered and
have the courage to be soft and in their hearts.

PARENTS RESPONSIBILITY WITH RITES OF PASSAGE

What is not generally understood is the role of the parent
while a young person goes through a rite of passage. Once
the youth returns they are no longer a child, they have passed
through a threshold, they are changed. This does not mean
they are a fully-fledged adult by any means, they are a young
adult. As they embark on this journey they require more
space to grow.

With our children we tend to hold them in a small field of
both experience and expectation. At the transition point of a
rite of passage a transfer of responsibility for decision making
starts. Simultaneously a relationship of the discovery of the
young person's purpose is growing. The first encounter a
young person has with their relationship to their greater
purpose is a profound step on their path. However the
development of finding and following ones purpose is an
ongoing refinement that takes place over many years. These
changes have a powerful impact on the ongoing role of the
parents.

If the parents continue to hold their 'child' in the same way as before they are constricting their growth. A careful increase of space to allow the youth to make sovereign choices and to find their own way is required. Otherwise we are keeping them in a 'child' holding pattern that can be painful for them; it might assert our power over them. But it does not allow them to individuate.

One of my instructors was holding a rite of passage in my woodland. As the young people were due to return from living in shelters they had made for the past four nights, I first received a phone call from a colleague who was concerned that the parents could not get in touch with the instructor holding the rite of passage. I then received another call from a different colleague, with the same request. I reassured them both that all would be well. The parents had seen on the weather forecast that there were some high winds due that night. This had prompted them to be concerned for their 'children'. They were no longer children they now had the makings of being young adults. Four nights in a shelter of their own construction with only food they could forage, making a fire using a bow drill is a transformative experience. When you are creating your whole world from what is there in nature a quality of self-reliance and trust in nature is seeded that creates a powerful connection. I eventually arrived back on site and found the whole group curled up asleep on the ground around a large fire, it was a beautiful sight. The youths had asked the trees if any of them would blow down in the wind and they had said no. So they felt safe. This panicking of the parents is natural because the response to protect their children is still in play. The young people had developed a powerful connection and had taken their measure of the situation which was borne out by them all returning safely.

So as well as holding them more lightly we have an opportunity to let go of any vicarious ways we were living through them. To drop our expectations that will otherwise hold and shape our young people until we as the parent passes over to the other side.

For those of you that have lost a parent, aside from the ongoing grief that remains that can take many years to come to terms with, there may have been an experience of the energetic inheritance that occurs as a parent dies. It is a feeling of a veil lifting as all the energetic holding dissolves. All the hopes and dreams the should's and ought's the judgements and criticisms that were held by the parent are released. It is possible for this veil to start to be lifted consciously at a rite of passage by the parent if they are honouring the transition and aware of how they are energetically holding their progeny. Imagine how it would be to live without years of criticism and naysaying that can be endemic to our relationship with our parents. Replacing this with encouragement and ways to empower our youths.

I suspect we have all experienced as young adults returning to spend time with our parents how we can fall back in to childhood patterns around them. This is the result of a lack of parental letting go and an absence of our own rite of passage. How wonderful would it be to feel that we were empowering our youths and young adults when they spend time with us through our skilful awareness of these hither to unconscious holding patterns?

When the parents have not experienced a rite of passage it

can be difficult for them to fully support their children through this transition. In our current society it can be almost accidental how we might find the appropriate thresholds to cross.

Here is an account of a friend's recollection of his rites of passage from boy to man. The three thresholds he identifies as the transformative edges to becoming a man are very relevant. As many older men who have not consciously moved through these thresholds can feel isolated and still in their boy self. It illustrates how we can travel through life seeking the place to transform from boy to man, trying to find different ways to grow in to being a man.

My rites of passage (so far) - Alistair Mayor

My first initiatory experience was leaving home; which I did more dramatically than most, I remember my father's embrace as I boarded a truck to hitchhike south, not stopping to look back till I reached Sydney some 12 months later. I slayed many dragons, conquered many peaks, swam many rivers, and rescued a few maidens.
When I returned; I was still a boy.

I drank my way through university, disappointed after the education of the road and ended up in London to seek my fortune.
And still I was a boy.

I trained as a counsellor in a room full of women; exploring the womb, and the relationship.

I forged a new relationship with the feminine, and still I was a boy.

At least by now I had some idea what I was looking for. My true initiation had three parts; standing up to and expressing myself to my father, welcoming my first child into the world, and a process with initiated men. Before I told my father that my partner was pregnant, I spoke of some of the unexpressed sadness and anger which had accompanied my childhood. (Writing this now I see the unexpressed was the issue; sadness and anger an un-avoidable or even necessary consequence of growing up in western culture.) An unexpected consequence of me stepping into the world of men, is in some way, it released my father from his role. Allowing him to step into the place of grand-father and elder, which was a joy to see him playing with my children - a part of him I saw less often. And in relation to me; allowed him to bless and honour the path I'd taken.

For many men becoming a father is the only rite of passage they experience, which is a little late because they then have to deal with becoming a man and a parent at the same time - not easy especially with the shortage of guides. So, I guess this was me, finding my manhood and parenthood at the same time, at times it was messy (and again I think it probably needs to be), making the transition from the simplicity of the world of a child to the complexity of the world of the adult. I was lucky (not just luck) within this tumultuous time to find myself a male mentor. I started to explore and understand what rites of passage was all about. I'd heard about 'The Mankind Project,' I'd dismissed it; not for me, too expensive, until at a moment the time was right, I signed up, negotiated the cost and went.

What was it for me to be a man? What was holding me back?
What was man after all? no-one had really shown me.
These questions were met, I fought my way through,
breaking some of the chains, learnt something about integrity
and responsibility. And all importantly guided like I never had
been before, by men, by men who had been initiated, who
had claimed their own authority.
For many years i'd felt young, younger than I was.
Now I was the age I was, and I had a mission, I had claimed
my place in the world.
At last, I could stand shoulder to shoulder, I was a man.

All this reminds me of a line from a Levellers song; an
anthem of my later teenage years. 'My father when I was
younger, took me up onto the hill, we looked down on the
city smoke and felt the factories spill. This is where I come
when I want to be free. Well he never was in this life time and
these words stuck with me - there's only one way of life and
that's your own.'
And now as a father, adult, and a man I grapple with the line
between freedom and constraint, I understand my father's
predicament, and respect him for it.

Alistair Mayor Bsc, Couns. Dip, Dip. Sup. (MBACP)

Counselling & Psychotherapy Brighton & Lewes

With two other men I have been involved in the development
of a Men's Rites of passage in the last few years. To meet the
need for men to consciously make this transition, it is an
evolving process. It is a process that dissipates shame,
engenders a powerful understanding of the masculine, a
strong experience of brotherhood and a connection to the
ancestors. It is a foray to the edge an exploration of male

mystery to reclaim the dignity and goodness of the masculine.

THE DIFFERENCE BETWEEN MOTHERING AND FATHERING

I would like to open the conversation about the differences between mothering and fathering. This next section is not comprehensive but hopes to create greater awareness through raising this difference. This difference is often expressed by the fathers holding a broader field for the child to play in. The father has assessed the risk, and is aware that the child is relatively safe yet often the parameters can be broader than a mother would be happy with. The risk is being assessed in relation to the father's capability to react in response to the situation becoming dangerous. When held skilfully rules may be put in place to establish things like consent, and when an activity needs to stop. For example ' If you want to fight with that stick can you ask if that other boy would like to play with you before attacking him' or introducing a 'pause button' or some signal at which point things need to calm down. This can be as simple as just saying 'pause' or 'freeze'. Similarly the whole activity could be carried out in slow motion, to develop the necessary dexterity.

A great deal of conflict can occur between mothers and fathers when the idea of parenting is totally mother or father centric. Bearing in mind the care of the child out of necessity is initially very mother centric for the early years. We also need to remember that there are plenty of mothers who are just as happy holding a larger field for their children as there are fathers who are overly cautious.

When we understand that mothering and fathering can be different it becomes possible to talk about these differences in parenting styles and hopefully come to a greater understanding of our partners actions and motivations and allow both mothers and fathers to find their more natural ways of rearing their children.

5

LIFE

We live increasingly stressful lives with less and less nature and human connection and we seem to have moved far away from nature and the natural. When we do move towards human connection we can be overcome by social anxiety, and a walk in the park can be all we have access to as far as connecting with nature is concerned. We are becoming more and more atomised, in our families, relationships work and play.

How do we bring more flow and connection into our daily lives? When we are in the Alpha state we are calm and focused, allowing any social anxiety to be diminished, and helping us to flow with our interactions and encounters.

As well as the Alpha breath dynamics practice, that brings us in to Alpha within two minutes and reconnects us with the flow, there are other approaches we can add to this that can enhance our flow state and increase connection.

SIT SPOT

The first is called a sit spot and is an integral aspect of nature connection practice. We choose a natural spot, perhaps at the bottom of our garden. Where we can sit and observe nature. This can be greatly enhanced by a mentor asking relevant questions that help to direct our awareness.

As we sit at different times of day and night and different times of year, we become aware of the baseline of our patch. Not realising at first how we can then use this information wherever we are. My understanding of bird alarm calls and behaviour that I learned in English woodlands at my sit spot has kept me safe when tracking leopards in India.

A simple experiment that can be run is to go to a chosen sit spot and practice the Alpha breath dynamics and see what effect this has on the bird life. When we are in an Alpha state we create fewer disturbances as our brainwave state is closer to the natural Schuman frequency. Our day can be uplifted wonderfully when birds come and sing around us. It can have a powerful effect on our sense of joy. The Alpha breath dynamics boosts our sit spot experience, bringing us to the realm of experienced sit spot practitioner as we attune to nature more swiftly.

Sit spots are now being included in some nature based therapy and their value is recognised by other branches of psychotherapy and psychology for the benefit they give in allowing us to process the difficult experiences we go through in life.

There are many ways we can use the sit spot; we can listen and learn about the birds, we can look at the tracks left by the animals that move through the area, we can learn about the plants growing in and around our spot, seeing them at all different times of year, we can use it for meditation and as a tool for reflection as well as observation. Perhaps we take a pressing question to our sit spot and see what is offered as a reflection or response from the natural world. We can also use the sit spot to awaken our senses and through this process expand our sensory capacity.

We could just as easily use our dog walking as a dynamic sit spot. Perhaps our trip to the park with the children could have an element of this for us, or maybe we are a keen gardener and our time in the garden is this meditative moment in our week. We may already be using these times in nature in a similar way as it is natural for us to seek out these moments of time out of time and in connection.

GRATITUDE

Gratitude is not something that can really be taught. How we each reach out with our mind and heart to thank all the people and things that support our life is a personal thing. Gratitude brings the recognition that we are not separate, not alone, that we are supported in so many ways. It is an antidote to disconnection.

I started to run camps for families in 2000 in order to teach parents and children the skills of survival and nature connection. This was because I was contacted by several single mothers who berated me for not offering courses that they could bring their children to and so the family camp was born in response to their feedback. Many of these single mothers are now very skilful and respected senior teachers of these skills and have been running their own schools for many years.

I used to start the camp with an exploration of the elements, Earth, Air, Fire and Water asking each participant to choose an element they felt they resonated with. Next we would figure out the compass directions, and then create an arrangement where each direction had an element; we were creating our own medicine wheel.

We would take each element for example fire and find all the things that we associated with this element; the sun, our capacity to cook, warmth, light, illumination, enlightenment and birth, as when it rises we wake up, other stars and the stories they carry.

Then we would feel which position to put each one in, perhaps for fire the east as that is where the sun rises and so on. Once this was complete I would ask if we could do without any of these elements. The children's response would be that we could not. I would mention how they were giving to us the whole time, the air we breathe, the water that makes up around eighty percent of us and our world, the earth that our bodies are made from, and even the phosphorous in our bones that is not made on earth, but in the stars.

Then I would ask how do we respond when we were given a gift? We say thank you they would reluctantly respond. Then this would begin our thanksgiving for the start of the camp. Referencing all the aspects that had been mentioned and turning and facing each direction in turn. There is an invitation for you to go through this process yourself and make your own personal way of giving thanks for the aspects that support your life. This is an ancient practice and you will find gratitude is rooted in all religious traditions.

At the times when we are struggling with life the most, these are the best times to give thanks the act of thanks giving can move us through the suffering. Even giving thanks for the challenges that life is presenting us with can change our relationship to those things allowing us to move from the victim role to a place where we have restored our capacity for choice. As choice is the enemy of victimhood.

I came across a powerful passage in Eidith Eigers book entitled 'The Choice'. She was made to dance for Mengele in Auschwitz, and while dancing understood that she was free and the soldiers were all trapped and overcome by the evil they were perpetuating. At a certain point in Auschwitz many of the Jews were dying and there was nothing to eat, and she witnessed some people turning to cannibalism. Instead she would go and sit on the grass and choose which blade of grass to eat. This is a powerful expression of not falling in to victimhood in the face of extreme tyranny.

Gratitude came in to focus as a transformative teaching for me when I experienced expressing gratitude in my sit spot. This changed the relationship of the birds and animals to my presence. The teaching I received presented gratitude as a technology that creates an internal state change that then flows out into nature. The birds and animals will respond to us differently when we give thanks, and this indicates the quality of state change that this brings us into. When our heart opens in this way it is felt by nature and nature is life. So this resonance flows out and affects our whole life.

I suggest that this is run as an experiment to see the difference this creates, to the sit spot experience.

Try this experiment: give thanks every morning for a week and see what effect this has on your life. It is crucial that you lift these ideas off the page and try them out otherwise you will never know if what is written here is true or not.

My first experience of genuine gratitude that went beyond it being a technique was with my daughter many years ago when she was four. It was a really hot day and Amber my daughter and I were playing together just enjoying each other's company. At one point Amber turned to me and filled with the joy of the moment let me know that she was happy to be with me without her mother there. This was a deeply moving moment for me as I was looking after her half of the time as a single father, having separated from her mother two years before. It was moments after this that a bee came past and stung her on the thumb. She went from joy to hysteria in less than sixty seconds. I was stunned too as it felt like the beauty of the moment was shattered by the venom of this tiny bee. We moved down the hill to our camp and as we went I remembered that the day before while in the woods harvesting some 'green' Ash for working with my pole lathe, I had come upon a patch of Burdock.

"Ah a healing plant to harvest for when it is needed, I think it is good for stings" I had thought and collected some leaves asking the plant politely. I had dried them out on the dash board of my car and as we came down the hill I suddenly remembered that they were specifically good for bee stings. I checked with my teacher's herbal "Tom Brown's field guide to edible and medicinal plants" and it suggested chewing up the leaves to put them on a bee sting. So began the task of chewing and rehydrating the Burdock leaf, to break up the cell walls and make the active compounds accessible.

Burdock is a very bitter leaf they can be eaten when very young but very quickly become bitter as they get older. These were not young leaves. So I began chewing making all kinds of sour faces. Then I put my chewing's on Amber's thumb. The first dollop of green pulp fell straight off. So I began to chew another leaf. Similar sour faces and much chewing later, the same thing unfortunately happened again and the precious dollop ended up on the ground for the second time. "Third time lucky?" I thought, while chomping on another Burdock leaf. This time I wrapped the chewed pulp in a whetted leaf and carefully wrapped it round her thumb. Inside a minute her whole countenance changed she forgot about the sting and went back to playing. It was at this point that a wave of gratitude came over me, for the Burdock plant.

I had been instructed to give thanks when harvesting wild plants and up till that point had done so just in word. From then on I meant it, I was actually on my hands and knees giving thanks to the burdock plant after that experience and this really changed the quality of my thanksgiving as a whole. What really makes the difference is when we can really feel the thanks as well as speaking the words.

My sense is that there is for each of us a pivotal moment that can change an exercise an experiment in to something far more. It may seem like a little thing at the time but the reality of that experience, where we receive something that was really wanted or needed provokes this type of genuine out pouring of feeling. Then our relationship to thanksgiving becomes real.

JOURNALING

The next aspect is journaling, and we might even combine this with the sit spot at times. Journaling is helpful in many ways, it externalises what we are experiencing and feeling and can help us work through what we are feeling. It then gives us a record of both powerfully positive shifts that can happen for us and difficult times. We can then be reminded of the triumphs when we are low and see how far we have come. Or perhaps catch the issues that keep coming up again and again that we are not managing to work with skilfully yet. We can also note the insights that we gain and the inspirations. It is from my many hours of journaling that my first book emerged. I always carry a journal and some are filled with sketches and some with writing. When I read my early journals, they are not like a diary, more like a record of the struggles and themes of what I was facing and working with. Rereading them allows the perspective to fully digest the experiences and then to make meaning from them. When we clearly see the loops of experience we are caught in our attention can flag up these behaviours when the y re-occur. Helping us to notice when we start down the same path and perhaps correcting it this time. If we can quieten the voice that wants to berate us for repeating the same mistakes and can learn from them. We can then transform these experiences which are often obstacles to understanding.

When I encounter accounts of beautiful experiences many times I have forgotten them and am delightfully reminded of those uplifting times. The capacity to write poetry has also emerged from the practice of journaling.

Here is a recent poem from my journal: 10/12/2019

Heart Grown

Born of rain and thunder

Of this sweet earth cracked asunder,

The spark of life blown in to existence

By the four winds careful insistence

This spirit self, a divine particle,

Glowing with love, and totally inseparable,

Together my love, we walk the same way

Each on our unique journey

Of eternal return,

Back to the source

If we let the flow of life run its course

Like the leaping salmon

Returning to spawn

But where is our home I hear you morn

Home is where the heart shines bright

Sun like at noon, not held like a hickory nut in the night

Then we do not die alone,

We die to the state our heart has grown.

At times I have also written many of these positive experiences on separate pieces of paper and put them in a big jar and when I was feeling down picked one or two out of the jar to remind myself what an amazing life this is.

THE OBSTACLE IS THE WAY

When we are in the midst of difficulties or cannot see past them the idea that the obstacle is the way may not be easy to accept. As we often try to push away the states we don't like and put off the tasks we have to do that we don't want to do. This pushing away of the states only makes them stronger. We can also try to avoid the steps we might need to take to accomplish a particular task and because of this avoidance make the completion of the task much harder or take much longer. This happens in the most practical of circumstances as well as the most existential.

In practical circumstances the key is often paying attention to the sequence of events and remaining flexible when things don't go according to plan.

I ran a festival for ten years and learned how to be flexible as things would always not go according to plan. It was very easy, in this high stress situation to loose ones emotional centre and so I choose to look upon it as a test of my level of meditation. If I could go through the whole festival from start to finish without getting upset then I knew my meditation was good.

Practically there were many things to sort out, and often amenities or caterers or musicians would unavoidably cancel. So being ready to go back to the beginning and start again, ringing round or searching the internet to find what was needed at the last minute was always a possibility.

One year we decided to create a one way traffic flow to help all the people living locally. We sent them all a letter to inform them and put this information in to our traffic management plan with a request for the police to inform us if we needed to do anything further.

On the day we were about to put up the signs I got a call from the local traffic police, explaining that someone had complained about the one way system we were going to institute and that we did not have the correct authorisation, it would have required us submitting a request months before to the appropriate authority. So as I spoke to the officer I explained that our intention was to create a clear traffic flow so the local inhabitants could have unencumbered access to their homes. This was creating a serious obstacle to festival access.

My experience with the responsible authorities up to this point was that they were always helpful and supportive. The question I then asked the officer was "what can we do about this", there was a pause and his response was "You can write voluntary on the signs". By directly engaging with the problem and asking someone who knows the ways around such matters we had a win. I was coming along side this officer who was phoning me to tell me not to put the signs up and instead he explained how we could proceed with our plan and act lawfully.

On an emotional note many people would turn up having had complex and sometimes difficult experiences on the way to the festival. They would come and find me because I was in charge and want to tell me their whole story, the drama of their journey. In this circumstance my band width for hearing distressing stories was diminished. We had many lovely people at the festival and a healing area and this was the place to take such stories. I would have to say, when the festival is over and I am sat round the fire that is the time to tell me a story, right now I just need to know what help you require.

If they shared directly their obstacle I could deal with it easily. The need to share the story was creating a further obstacle, for them it was a justification for whatever their request was. In most instances I was happy to grant their request without the need for justification.

This then brings us to how we relate to negative emotional states. The normal situation is that they come and we have to deal with them and our emotional state fluctuates between good and bad and this is considered normal. When we actually start to develop a relationship with our negative emotions this can change. We start to learn our emotional states like a skill. We develop strategies to put in place that help us work with these states.

Using the Alpha breath dynamics is one such strategy as it creates a balanced emotional flow. That can diminish the peaks and troughs we can put ourselves through or help to reset our emotional state when it has dipped returning us to calm and focused.

TRANSFORMING NEGATIVE EMOTIONS

There are other strategies that work for different emotions and the principle is to understand what the emotional state robs us of. For example when we are depressed we struggle to focus, we cannot commit, we find it hard to be definite, to choose a course of action.

I am an ardent flint knapper; (Knapping is shaping flint, by hitting it with stones and antler hammers to make useful artefacts) I have found that when I used to get depressed, I would go and break some stones, by flint knapping. Within half an hour my state would have changed. This happened multiple times until I had to deconstruct what was actually happening. I realised that in order to make a stone object, several crucial things were required. Focus, precision, clear decision making and commitment. Within the half an hour it took to change my state it would not matter if I managed to make anything useful or not it was only the specific set of actions that had the effect of changing my state.

There are many other activities that have similar characteristics. One is drawing sacred geometric shapes, or flower arranging, playing chess or making a playlist. The activity is not important just that it has the necessary characteristics that the emotional state robs you of.

Journaling is excellent for helping with self-doubt as we look back at past triumphs we can be reminded of how we moved through difficult situations in the past and this can give us the perspective we have lost.

Shame is a very low emotional frequency, as the feeling creates a negative self-consciousness and removes confidence, separating our sense of self from feeling accepted and loved. We can feel that what has generated the feelings of shame are unique to us, that we are the only one that has ever perpetuated the action or created the situation we feel shame about. So we hide this feeling away rather than expose it to anyone. This only makes it have more power over us. When we feel ashamed we are struggling with self-acceptance and if we can share what we feel shameful about with others that will accept us, then the power of the shame is diminished.

Perhaps we know a patient wise friend that we can share in confidence with or we can talk to a therapist. As bringing the light of awareness on to theses darker areas helps them to shift. The secretive nature of shame can eat us from the inside or be shared and diffused.

We often fear being judged and shunned, yet it is in the act of sharing and expressing ourselves that the shame starts to lessen its grip.

An experiment to try is to share some dark secret or difficult emotional issue not with other humans but just out in nature with the forest. You will be surprised to find a huge sense of relief and then the arrival of possible answers to your conundrums in ways you did not expect.

I have sat in many sharing circles and when people share in

confidence the things that are eating away at them there is almost every time someone in the circle who has had a similar experience. In the vulnerability of sharing these difficulties comes greater inner strength, and mutual respect. We can even give permission to others to share their difficult inner experiences by sharing our vulnerabilities. When we are asked to speak in front of a group of people we might be feeling nervous. If we share this vulnerability we clear the air for ourselves emotionally and can find that the group can be more supportive.

THE TRANSFORMATIONAL POWER OF ART

Some of these feelings are so rooted in our being that we may need different strategic approaches to work with them. Art has the capacity to transform our difficult emotional energies into something beautiful.

In the process of experiencing grief, there is a delicate and sometimes lengthy transformation that can take place, of the grief of loss into praise for that which we have lost. This can be expedited through poetry, painting, dance or any creative process. Many great masterpieces from songs we love to paintings and poems can be the artist working out these feelings. It is possible to realise that this is a universal process and that our skill with grief is a really important one to be well practiced at.

Here is a poem dedicated to my father who died over 25 years ago:

Missing star

It is not death we fear,
It is the loss of the idea of our story of separation,
Our individual story,
That makes us stand out from the back ground,
And one by one we toss out masks off the cliff edge,
Back in to the mystery,
Until all that is left is the original face,
We are each a unique bead
Threaded on to the necklace of the divine,
And those who have left this reality
Leave a space
Like a missing star in our favourite constellation,
Each being,
Like each raindrop travels along its own track,
Flowing with inevitability back
To the unknowable from where it came.

To Stephan

GET ACTIVE

The next strategy is to get active, when we run or engage in
yoga, dance or sport we generate endorphins. This is a
chemical release in the body that creates a cascade of positive
change. As we expend energy we generate the capacity for
more energy to enter the body.

Perhaps we choose to do a physical job that needs doing as if it were our physical training rather than putting it off. Then we also get the feeling of accomplishment once the job is done.

I recommend that when turning to exercise to change our mood we start gently and work our way up to our full capacity.

MAKING A GESTURE

I had a friend when I lived in Bristol who would always come round in a very depressed state. I liked this friend but found after his visits I would be left carrying his depression having often taken up hours of my time to be present for him. So I decided to make a gesture with him. I came up with what I considered to be a win-win strategy for us both.

The next time he came to my door I said 'Ah John I'm just going for a run would you like to join me?'. The first time this happened he declined and left and I went back to the kitchen table sat down and continued to drink my tea.

This happened again a second time and he declined my offer to go for a run and so I continued doing what I was doing.

It was on the third time he came to the door perhaps a week later and again I said 'Ah what a coincidence, John I'm just about to go for a run would you like to join me?'. 'I don't have any running shoes on' he said. I suggested we could jog to his house where he could pick up some running shoes and we could go from there. So we set off, once he had his shoes on we began jogging. This took at least an hour and a half and his house was only five minutes away.

As we moved to the outskirts of Bristol towards open country we encountered an area strewn with litter. I could not pass it by without doing something about it and began to pick the litter up finding a large bag and beginning to fill the black bag with litter. My friend who was an environmental activist was both shocked and delighted to discover that it was possible to make a small difference to the environment whilst on a jog. We filled a large black bag with rubbish and found a bin to deposit it in and continued on our way. Once we got back his mood was buoyant and cheerful we shared a cup of tea and then I went home.

The fourth time he came to my door I said 'Hey John I'm going for a run do want to come?' He replied' yea sure'. So off we went with the same outcome as before. The next time he came to my door he was no longer depressed he seemed cheerful energised and full of life and I invited him in for a cup of tea.

I had made a gesture with my friend without criticising or saying anything I had just shown him how to change his emotional state and to build some energy.

FACE THE DEMON

All of these approaches so far are ways of changing our state rather than facing the emotion head on. One of the most useful approaches is firstly to choose the most difficult emotion to face and develop a direct relationship with it.

This then develops our capacity and skill in relating to the arrival of any negative emotion. If we choose fear as perhaps the most difficult emotion to face and decide that whenever it shows up we ask, "What have you come to teach me this time?" we are engaging in a win-win strategy. Because we will either learn something from the appearance of this emotion or it will spontaneously disappear.

When we learn to skilfully relate to emotion it does not matter if it comes or not as we know how to relate to it. This process does not necessarily happen straight away it may take a few applications to develop enough understanding, to be less affected by the particular emotion. Give yourself plenty of space to experiment multiple times with as little self-criticism as possible. Remember the outcome of your playful experiment is feedback. Whether you consider it good or bad is not the issue but whether you learned from it.

We are engaged in changing a habit so this can take quite a few attempts for our behaviour to change.

Step one is to observe what is going on. Gurdjieff called it: 'park dog duty', as if you are sat on a bench watching the dog frolic about in the park. (The dog in this instance being the behaviour you want to change which is most often some activity of the mind.)

Step two is to catch yourself as soon after the process has happened as possible.

Step three is to catch yourself earlier on in the process.

Step four is catching yourself in the act as the process is happening.

The final step is to catch yourself before you express the behaviour.

If we enlist a playful attitude we will find it takes far fewer attempts to change our behaviour.

LEANING IN

We can also decide to go with the emotion and immerse ourselves in it rather than fight it. I have found this to be very useful as again the pushing away of the feeling can make it stronger. It then loses its power as most of the power of a negative emotion is bound up with us rejecting it rather than the choice to lean in to it. When a feeling of self-pity arises and we start sulking, if we really go in to the sulk we can find it shifts much sooner. As we lean in we start to exaggerate the feeling and this leads to a light self-parody that can break the spell of the feeling.

GUT BRAIN AXIS

There is growing evidence that gut health and brain health are inextricably interwoven. The gut brain axis is a two way communication between the cognitive and emotional centres of the brain and the peripheral intestinal functions. This means that what is going on in the gut affects brain and emotional function. The types of conditions that are being looked at in this context are autism and anxiety-depressive behaviours as the conditions that are most effected by gut imbalance. Faecal transplants, that increase the gut microbiome, are being researched to treat these disorders.

This suggests that some mental conditions could be treated with the introduction of certain bacteria and enzymes. The other link with our gut microbiome is with the soil. If our soils are getting depleted of their natural microbes and we are growing our food in them it stands to reason that this will reduce our gut microbiome too. This starts to make a case for organic food production and consumption to aid mental health. If we are eating denatured food then we are actively depleting our gut microbiome.

As well as the microbial input what we eat can change our mood and state. We have all experienced a sugar rush and the subsequent energy and emotional trough that can follow. Also certain drinks affect brainwave states: green tea can induce an Alpha state, wine a Theta state, (hence how it can make us sleepy.) Coffee can put us in to the faster brainwave state of Beta.

Posture is another factor. When we adopt a slumped posture our internal organs get compressed and their function is impaired, yet when we are holding a good posture both our internal organs and mental state can function well. As a teenager my father would always correct my posture which I found really annoying. Until I ran some experiments and found when I made the effort to hold a good posture I felt a lot better. It was an effort to start with came with quite a lot of discomfort. By maintaining a good posture the discomfort eventually disappeared along with the negative emotional feelings and it became my natural posture.

CONNECTION WITH NATURE, SELF AND OTHER

One of my students and now colleagues, an ex-army sergeant major, attended a nature connection class I ran many years ago. During this week long class I witnessed a fascinating reintegration of his experience. He had been out of the army for around four years and had put his twenty two year army career behind him. He is also the most experienced bird watcher I have ever met.

During the course I saw all his life experience reintegrate as we were working with Apache scout skills, bird language and other nature connection practices and games. He left the course glowing and on a new trajectory. He was working at the time in a 12 step addiction centre. There he began to use the nature awareness games as a therapeutic intervention. By slowing the exercised down and allowing more time to explore what came up for his clients, the nature connection games became a therapeutic intervention. Obviously holding a safe space to explore the issues that arose takes skill and training. Using one simple game of "meet a tree" he would get the addicts to step three of the twelve step program. He later studied to become a psychotherapist and now works with Nature therapy.

The overriding shift that I have witnessed is that when we are disconnected from ourselves, it is possible by connecting with nature to re-find that connection to self and others.

When we go to our sit spot or play with the nature awareness games we are connecting with the natural world which is benign, non-critical and accepting. Perhaps we are able to find a tree that we have only been lead to whilst being blind folded, or we hear a bird sing close by, or spot some newly opened flower. All these things create connection with nature and bring positive feelings in to our system. This can then allow us to enjoy connecting with the self again, as perhaps our experience was painful before. Or we were struggling to accept some part of the self and the mirror of nature shows us where we are in a non-judgemental way. Primarily our road to connection with others is then clearer as we can be feeling better about ourselves, perhaps more accepting or having been uplifted by our experience. At a secondary level we may also have a story of connection and wonder to share.

PRIMARY RELATIONSHIP

Our primary relationship is with ourselves. So perhaps it is worth us getting to know ourselves well and working through the various resistances we might have. For example we might be afraid of the dark. We are going to spend half of our lives in the dark so we might as well develop a good relationship with darkness. Knowing ourselves is an ongoing project as we are evolving and changing. The more we know ourselves the more authentic we can be.

While in relationship with another this understanding that our primary relationship is with ourselves is important to bear in mind. We can easily let this go and become too entwined with the other and not be able to recharge our own energy. Creating the right balance of time with the self and time together will bring more emotional space allowing time to process and reflect.

We can also override our own guidance and feelings. If we were to listen to ourselves and act from a place of our inner knowing, our inner compass, we would be able to remain more centred and whole. When we override ourselves it is as if we cut off part of the self that gets excluded from the relationship and slowly we diminish ourselves in order to remain in the connection with the other.

BODY COMPASS

Wouldn't it be fantastic if we had a way of knowing if things are going to work out well for us? If we had some way of filtering out the noise, zeroing in on what would serve us best in this world of immense choice, leading us to the best outcome.

This is where body compass comes in, once honed it can help us to make life and death decisions as well as find our lost car keys. Sounds like quite a claim, yet as usual no belief is necessary, but diligence is required.

I am going to suggest several experiments that can get your body compass up and running. Then you can start running multiple experiments with short feedback loops to be able to get clear readings from your body compass.

Your body responds directly to certain situations to warn you or tell you all is well. For example you are walking in to a party or a bar and suddenly you feel a gut wrenching feeling that you should not be there, something is not right or about to kick off. Or you meet someone and feel a powerful sense of release and ease as if everything is in its place. These natural feelings are how your body communicates with you. It is with this natural facility in the body that we are going to develop the capacity to communicate. By asking simple yes and no questions and then feeling the response in the body we can develop a two way conversation with our body compass.

To calibrate this we need to find questions we know the answers to. We start the process by asking ourselves a question where we know the answer is a NO. Like "would I lick a dog turd" this will trigger a strong response in the body and create a tightening in some area of the body. Once we have asked our question (that does not have to be this one) we scan the body for a response. We locate the place where we had a feeling of tightening or discomfort.

Next we find a question we know the answer is a YES. We ask ourselves this question and then scan the body for a feeling of release. This usually happens in the same place. To increase the effectiveness of this experiment I recommend you practice the Alpha breath dynamics first. This is because our inner compass can be fogged by a lack of inner clarity. So any form of meditative practice will help to clarify the results of the inner compass.

Once this facility is established use it in a playful way. Use it to decide which café to have a coffee in. If you are meeting someone check to see if they will be on time or late. If you lose something use your yes and no questions to your compass to narrow down where to look.

It can take some time to calibrate but once it is up and running you can use it for far greater decisions. This practice is similar to kinesiology, but run in an internal way.

As a Libran when I was introduced to this it was a complete God send as up to that point I had difficulty choosing between tea and coffee. I had experienced a great deal of indecision prior to learning this practice and so I set about developing my inner compass with gusto. When I really started to get clear readings I began to rely on it more and more. I remember going to visit a friend with my then partner. We rang the bell and there was no answer, we had been invited round at that time so were perplexed that they did not seem to be in. My partner suspected that they had popped out to the shops and so went to sit on the sunny side of the street. I asked my inner compass if they were in and got a yes that they were in, so I continued to ring the bell. Eventually they came to the door. They had been vacuum cleaning in a back room in the house and could not hear the doorbell. So I have used it for such frivolous things as well as making life and death decisions relying on my inner compass.

6

FINAL WORD

It is my intention that this book is read and that it inspires practice and experimentation. If you have just read through without trying the various exercises then I invite you to go back to which ever section is most relevant and find an exercise to try (especially the Alpha Breath Dynamics).

Remember approach each exercise playfully. Have no expectation, and regard all results as feedback rather than as good or bad.
Practicing the Alpha Breath Dynamics at home is a good start. You might also head into a nearby area of nature and practice and see how the birds and animals respond to your presence.
This whole approach is not about believing what is written here it is about having your own experience and building on that. The encouragement is to follow your own lines of inquiry that lead you to a deeper understanding of the mystery that is life.

We can feel quite bewildered when we are presented with a different perspective. There can be many new things to learn and new experiences to be had. We can feel inadequate and overwhelmed by the many choices.

So let's slow down and take a breath.

We can look at all the possibilities as if we have many new adventures to go on. These adventures will lead us into a clearer view of ourselves and the situations and nature that surround us. Then we can proceed to unwrap each experience like a child on Christmas day unwraps their presents. Coming to each experiment with excitement and joy, rather than wishing we had already solved all of our problems. We can apply this principle to any new situation.

I have shared some of my stories here and hope they have been helpful and illustrative. I also look forward to hearing some of your stories of how you have used the skills and practices in this book to run your own experiments and the results of your practice.

Many Blessings

Thomas Schorr-kon 2/11/21

ABOUT THE AUTHOR

Thomas Schorr-kon is an international teacher and author.
He has been teaching for 25 years through his school
wwwtrackways.co.uk.
His first book 'True Nature' chronicles many of the skills and
experiences he teaches.
His warrior of the heart courses follow an in depth process of
creating inner freedom and peace. Touching on many of the
aspects mentioned in this book.
He trained as a martial artist since the age of 8 and started to
meditate in his early teens. He was the first to bring the
Nature connection teachings to the U.K. and has trained
thousands of students several of whom were responsible for
bringing John Young to the U.K.
He ran a festival for ten years to help to build community and
has now helped to set up the first of several regenerative and
re-wilding farms.

Printed in Great Britain
by Amazon